Why the Long Face?

Why the Long Face?

The Adventures of a Truly Independent Actor

Craig Chester

St. Martin's Press ☙ New York

www.stmartins.com

Library of Congress Cataloging-in-Publication Data

Chester, Craig.
    Why the long face? : the adventures of a truly independent actor /
Craig Chester—1st ed.
        p. cm.
    ISBN 0-312-28713-5
    1. Chester, Craig, 1965–   2. Actors—United States—Biography.
I. Title.

PN2287.C5355 A3 2003
792'.028'092—dc21
[B]

                                                    2002031884

First Edition: January 2003

10   9   8   7   6   5   4   3   2   1

For Michael Stremel and Erazmus, the cat

Contents

Acknowledgments

During the writing of this book I realized something—writing is quite different from acting. There is no audience to clap or laugh or cheer you on at the end of the night, no hair and makeup people to powder and style you before you sit down in front of your computer screen when you begin your writing day.

While not comprising a traditional audience, there were plenty of tenderhearted souls whose cheers, support, and laughter kept me going for the year or so it took to create what you are about to read.

I'd like to thank my editor, Michael Connor; my phantom editor and soul sister, Parker Posey; also Elizabeth Beier, Ben Rogers, Thomas Beller, Joanna Yas, Jackie Beat, Katherine Connella, George Hahn, Kerry Barden, Mike Albo, Steve Lippman, John Krokidas, Ned Stresen-Reuter, Brian Sloan, Craig Miller, Nora Burns, Peter Kouzmov, Meg Bowles, John Turner, Mark Fowler, Illeana Douglas, John Cameron Mitchell, Lisa LoCicero, Tom Kalin, Craig Paul, Daniel Garcia,

Zeke Farrow, P.L. Moore, Andersen Gabrych, John Polly, Mark Tusk, Nora Burns, Chip Duckett, Melissa Mobley, Michael Panes, Hannah Minghella, Tom Soluri, Sarah Fargo, Roseanne Quezada, Michael Cunningham, Bruce Steele, Dennis Hensley, Paula Malcomson, David Pevsner, Ilo Orleans, Mark Bennett, Pauley Perrette, Alonso Duralde, Dave White, Laurie Ochoa, Jesse Dorris, Neil Olsen, and especially my amazing and talented literary agent, Edward Hibbert.

But mostly I would like to thank my family: Kim, who is the epitome of sweet little sisterhood; Linda, for teaching me empathy and the curative powers of love; and my father, Cecil, who sold bags of catfish fry on the side of a highway so he could send me money in New York because I was struggling to become an actor and was hungry.

Where's Your Top?

Dottie looked fifties. She was, for a girl born in 1966, some-what unnaturally preoccupied with the generation that pre-ceded hers and she took to that carefree decade's mind-set like a poodle to a skirt. For a girl whose life goal was the confining margins of 1950s housewifery, Dottie was undeni-ably out of sync with the times. It was, after all, 1976 and while women were burning their bras defiantly, Dottie counted the days till she would fill her very own darts. She was fabulous and kooky but mostly she was just fifties.

Before I knew that "camp" meant *Valley of the Dolls* and *Whatever Happened to Baby Jane?*, that four-letter word in-spired ominous dread. Church camp, in case you don't know, has nothing to do with gay men lip-syncing to "Amazing Grace" in Virgin Mary garb. There are no aging Christian actresses, no eye-rolling at audaciously bad line readings from the Bible—none of the irony that word would later embody for me.

As a child, "camp" meant being ripped from the safe bosom

of my doting mother and thrust into the mosquito-infested, Scripture-ridden swamps and lakes scattered throughout California and later Texas. Like Meryl Streep's little girl in *Sophie's Choice*, I would be loaded into a windowless railroad car with all the other doomed and damned children of the world, and away I would go, shipped off to a Born Again Kinderlagen for two-week stretches of internment.

On my first ride to Kidshwitz, huddled next to Rosa Parks in the back of the bus, I gazed at the wondrous creation that was Dottie as she held court up front. En route, I began strategizing how I might survive this two-week wrongful conviction.

I always felt that on some level I was a blousy old actress shoved into the effeminate body of a small boy. I never really liked any of the other kids, mostly because they didn't particularly care for me. I desperately wanted their *attention*, if not necessarily their *company*, and I find that maddening dichotomy to be true of myself even today.

But on that day, I wanted nothing more than Dottie's attention—to be near her, to bask in the glow of her luminescent incarnation. I was the only boy in an extended family of all-girl cousins, aunts, and the like. Our family gatherings resembled a casting call for a trailer-park production of *Little Women*. But Dottie was different from my cousins or my aunts—she was glamorous, full of confidence, and she had that cool 1950s look to boot.

"Did you watch *Laverne and Shirley* last night?!" she squealed to her entourage of girlfriends. "Oh my gosh, I was, like, totally there when they filmed that episode. We met Shirley and Squiggy after the show, they signed my Boo Boo Kitty doll!" she boasted.

Shirley Feeney was Dottie's false god and I wondered what

Cindy Williams, the actress, had thought of this ten-year-old miniature version accosting her backstage on the Paramount lot.

Growing up in the suburban hellhole of California's San Gabriel Valley, I was always painfully aware of the fabulousness of Hollywood that glittered just over the hills. For those of us living *behind* the HOLLYWOOD sign, we knew the illusory qualities that symbol possessed—from the rear, the HOLLYWOOD sign is just a bunch of wood.

People in the Valley have a relationship to Hollywood very similar to that of Brooklynites with Manhattan. There is a feeling of not being quite whole—always living in the shadow of something greater, more amusing, and more important. Still, as a child so fascinated by television that I watched test patterns, I longed to go over that hill. To escape my predicament. I wanted to climb into the TV and play all the parts myself—and every color of the test pattern too.

As a boy, people often mistook me for a small girl from a far-off land, an exchange student, perhaps, from the country Androgomenea. Stifled by lip-zipping shyness, I rarely spoke to other children, although not for a lack of anything to say: bullies had beaten muteness into me and I shut up for fear of giving them brass knuckles.

Sporting longish straight black hair with china-doll bangs that I fought over tooth and nail with my parents, I was rarely seen as a boy, much to the dismay of my parents, who both fit perfectly into their allotted gender roles. My mother only wore dresses, cooked, cleaned, suffered longly, and never cussed. My father sported tattoos on his arms, drove with one wrist on the steering wheel, and watched football when he wasn't busting a gut over *Sanford and Son*.

Church camp was just one of many Herculean efforts by

my folks to socialize me as both a God-fearing Christian and pussy-whipped straight man. My parents had made me suspicious of other people, consistently bemoaning the fact that everyone else's families were a bunch of messed-up, untrustworthy nutcases who would screw your wife, kick your dog, and do *anything* to break up your happy home while dragging you to hell with them. The complete mistrust of non-Christians was counteracted by utter and blind faith in church and all of its devotees. The thought was that nothing, besides fear of prison time, could possibly rein in the wanton moral chaos of those with no concept of hell to regulate one's choices.

Since no one could be trusted, my options for playmates were limited. As a result, my only childhood friend was a retarded man named Brian. Brian was eighteen when I was eight, and while the May/December aspect of our friendship might seem a bit unusual, it was actually quite natural, being that Brian's mental capacity was somewhere near that of mine. We would play for hours, taking breaks to eat peanut butter and banana sandwiches his mom would make. He always smelled like peanut butter, bananas, and poop and he was my best friend. For years I thought I was retarded too since we were so much alike, and I'm certain some ex-boyfriends of mine might agree that I was on to something there.

Just before I had been shipped off to camp, my sister Kim and I had squeezed past the throng of onlookers at our suburb's Fourth of July parade. There, sitting on a sparkling white convertible, was actress Valerie Bertinelli.

One Day at a Time had debuted the night before and when I saw her, a jolt of electricity ran through me. She was being her perky little self, hand up, waving like an animatronic at Disneyland's Country Bear Jamboree. She was the first bona fide celebrity I ever saw in the flesh. She had come over the hills to the Valley, waving and spreading her joy to the smog-choked civilians. Valerie Bertinelli lived, worked, and played over the hill and I wanted to jump in her convertible, wave good-bye to my sister, and have Valerie carry me to a place where I could finally gaze upon the HOLLYWOOD sign as it was meant to be seen—from the front.

But there were no white convertibles in my childhood, just a bus to Big Bear Camp. And the Valerie Bertinelli of that camp, while certainly not as highly paid, was Dottie.

Dottie's popularity increased once we settled into the camp setting. Her log cabin was next to mine, and from my screen window I would hear her nightly laughter echo off the pine trees—that squeaky peal of delight unique to ten-year-old falsettos. I would lie in my cabin thinking about Dottie. I decided that she would be my friend no matter what and someday *I'd* be the one to get her to laugh that high-pitched cackle.

Olympic fever had made it all the way to Big Bear Mountain that year at camp. Shortly after arriving, we were instructed by camp counselor Steve that we would be participating in our own version of the Summer Olympics. Not only would we be competing in events, we would also make our own bronze, silver, and gold metals out of plaster of paris.

Counselor Steve was perhaps the most spectacularly handsome, sun-kissed specimen of male beauty I had ever seen. Dark hair that smiled slightly at the ends, tan and lean, he possessed a look that was unique to the time period—a look that I've only seen since in 1970s porn.

Steve also had the supernatural ability to make his heart stop on cue. This party trick was the talk of camp. While sitting around the dining hall Steve invited all those who were interested to press their head up against his chest and listen, while he closed his eyes and stopped his heart from beating for what seemed like forever. Then he would start it again, taking a deep breath, and everyone would scream with goose-bumped delight.

Dottie partook of Steve's party trick and squealed her squeaky laugh. Next it was my turn. Slowly I approached Steve. He pressed my ear up against his muscular chest, the warmth from his sunburn radiating onto my cheek. The *thump, thump, thump* gradually ceased. As he stopped his heart, mine started. His skin cooled slightly, then, just at that moment of panicked concern, it would beat again. I looked up at him and smiled. But inside I was squealing with Dottie-like glee.

After the ceramic Fauxlympic medals were spray-painted their colors of victory, the games began. Each of us was assigned to a team. I was assigned to the same team as Dottie—much to the chagrin of all else involved. Dottie sussed up the situation by talking to each of us individually.

"What event are you strong in?" was the first thing she ever said to me.

I stood there, stunned, not knowing how to respond. Instead I licked my lips in nervous concentration, a habit I was known for. After not responding for what seemed an eternity, Dottie straightened her kerchief and left me alone to my mute self, moving on, walking down the hill to her girlfriends. That she didn't push the envelope to get me to speak made me love her more.

It might be hard to imagine how one can navigate through a two-week camp setting, with its bonfires and marshmallow roasts, and never have one formal introduction, but that's exactly what I did. I had never been away from my mother and had no social skills whatsoever. Other than the necessity of "yes" and "no," I didn't say much. Looking back, I see that if I had started talking, I might never have stopped.

The day of the Big Bear Olympics arrived.

Having the athletic ability of a throw pillow, any mention of sports sends me running—well, actually *walking*—for cover. I have never understood this country's zealous addiction to sports. When I watch the news, I resent those ten minutes of annoying scores and what seem to me to be the same clip of the same person catching the same ball over and over again.

Having no idea what I could contribute athletically to my team, I stood on the sidelines while my other teammates jumped over poles and raced each other in potato sacks. My team was doing exceedingly badly, in desperate need of a gold medal to tip the scales.

Just then, what looked like a gigantic metallic boulder began rolling down the path towards us. It was a huge silver ball, quite durable and thick-skinned, yet essentially a big balloon. This challenge seemed to be the most difficult and right out of a science-fiction movie. Each child would, while the clock timed them, balance on the large globe. The one who remained on the ball the longest would win the coveted gold "medal."

One after the other, campers would climb aboard the ball, only to immediately go careening over the other side. This went on and on, with each member of my team undulating and tipping this way and that.

Suddenly something struck me. It was one of those moments of clarity I've read about in books endorsed by *The Oprah Winfrey Show*. I had no idea how I knew this, but I approached Dottie and actually spoke to her for the first time.

"I can do that," I said.

Everyone looked at me.

"Are you sure?" she said, hands on hips in worried consternation.

I approached Bob, the macho tattooed camp counselor I feared. Bob was a reformed Hell's Angel who had found Jesus and was now paying penance for the many children he had most certainly killed in his heyday. Surprised at my determination to climb on board, he grabbed my little hips and lifted me up, up, up until I perched atop the shining metallic ball six feet in the air.

And there I stayed—on hands and knees, perfectly centered and able. Through my navel ran an imaginary thread connecting me to the center of the earth. The minutes ticked on. There was a crisp, prolonged silence as Bob watched the hands on his watch. After five minutes, he called it a game. By this point I knew that I could balance on that ball till summer passed, the leaves buried me in fall, and the snow fashioned the globe and me into a perfectly proportioned snowman.

I climbed off the silver balloon as the entire camp—men, women, and children—cheered and clapped. Dottie came over, beaming.

"Oh my gosh!" She threw her arms around me. "You are so—swell!"

With that, a gold plaster-of-paris medal was wrapped around my neck and I was literally carried away by the crowd. I heard Dottie laughing her high-pitched laugh. Mission accomplished.

From that point on, I tagged along with Dottie everywhere. She told me everything about her life, her dreams, how she had kissed a boy in the woods. I mostly listened, nodding along supportively and conspiratorially. However, we never actually talked about me. I never even told her my name; I just glommed on to her, basked in her persona, and felt quite pleased with myself.

Near the end of summer camp I found my voice. Steve, the dreamboat camp counselor, asked me to go with him to fetch extra Bunsen burners for a cookout. Crossing through a thick, wooded forest, we walked for a good ten minutes back to a portion of the camp stocked with supplies and broken-down bunk beds. After loading up the bag of goods, we headed back to the campground in silence, through the thicket as the sun began to set.

As I walked with Steve, I felt strange. I had never been alone before with a grown man other than my father. Steve was beautiful and healthy and warm. He spoke to me with an inherent respect usually denied children by adults, and in my mind I saw him and me running off together, getting married, and watching him sleep on our honeymoon, all tan against the whiteness of our pristine sheets—sheets offered as a wedding present from my beaming parents. I never thought of Steve sexually per se, but my first gay feelings revolved around falling in love, cherishing someone, as opposed to sticking something into a hole. I forgot that I felt this way for many years, distracted as most gay men are when in their prime, but like most of childhood's lessons, I've returned to what I first knew.

Just inside the jungle of pine trees, we crunched on their needles until suddenly I noticed only the crunch of my own steps. I turned back to see Steve, as pale now as he had been tan only minutes before, clutching his arm in pain. He then clutched his chest, looked at me with a strange pleading look I had never seen before, or since, and fell onto the blanket of pine, in the throes of a full-fledged heart attack. I ran to him.

His eyes seemed dark, self-possessed to the point of blindness. I stood alone in the woods.

Terrified, and not knowing what to do, I dropped my bag and ran. I ran and ran and ran—my own heart in my throat—gasping for air and yelling, screaming, begging for my legs to move faster.

As I approached the clearing that comprised the campground, I could feel myself flying. I am certain to this day that I actually left the ground for a minute—the same way I had balanced on that ball for five. I saw all the children sitting at a picnic table. Bob, the Hell's Angel, hovered over them.

"Help! Help! Help!" I cried.

Bob approached me, taken aback and uneasy with the display of my emotion.

I struggled for words. I couldn't speak for lack of air. Finally I burst into a tearful rant, a hysterical, out-of-control, and frenzied rush of information.

"Steve had a heart attack! He's dead! He's lying in the woods! I saw him die! He looked at me and he fell down in the woods! He's out there and he's dea—"

Bob shook me. He shook me in that quickly repetitive way that adults shake children. My head snapped back. I swallowed my tongue and I saw the sky, discombobulated.

"Stop it! You're upsetting the other children!" he screamed.

Two other counselors sprinted into the woods to assist Steve. I looked around and Bob was right. The other children, who had also put their heads on the twenty-five-year-old Steve's heart and laughed as it stopped, were now crying. Many of them hugged each other and they looked scared and confused. I had upset the other children, but somehow, affecting them made me feel glad. They should know of such things, I thought. Such things exist.

An ambulance arrived an hour later. Steve clung to life and I never saw him again. Bob hated me from that moment on, not because I was upset by what I had experienced, but because I had shared it. I'm sure in his mind, my emotionalism had incriminated me as feminine, expressive in a way that defined me as weak in his macho eyes. But as Bob hated me—a boy, expressing fear—I grew to hate him right back. Because such things do exist and I don't want to be the only one aware of that fact.

Steve survived his heart attack, I found out later. He made a full recovery. But the glory of my gold medal had been quickly cut short by an emotional display that night. The other children resented my alarmism and felt intruded upon. Dottie was the only one who kept me close.

"He was so cute. Don't you think Steve's cute?" she asked me.

I couldn't believe this question. *How could she ask me that? She must know I want to marry him.* Not knowing quite how to answer that, I did what most children do when confronted with an uncomfortable issue and ignored it as we went off to play.

The last day of camp, all the children were loaded into a yellow school bus and taken on a fifteen-minute journey to a local indoor pool. "John Jacob Jingleheimer Schmidt" rang out loudly in the bus, but this time I sang along, comforted and validated by my new best friend Dottie, who had promised me her undying loyalty as friend, soul mate, and ally even after we were returned to our normal, sixth-grade lives. I hugged her gladly and sang along as we bounced over bumps in the dirt road on the way to go swimming.

Dottie and I had become great pals, albeit in a rather one-sided relationship. I never got an official introduction into her fold, the glory of the big silver ball being too dramatic a beginning for formal introductions of "Hi, my name is . . ." Still, ours was a nonverbal, nonprescribed kinship—we were above such mortal customs.

Inside the melee of the indoor pool's building, we were somehow separated. I happily went to the boys' changing room to get into my bright orange swim trunks with brown trim. When I exited the changing room, I was pleased to find Dottie already in the pool, treading water in a smart flowered swim cap. I jumped in the water to greet her, only to find a mortified Dottie staring back at me as I emerged.

"Where's your top?" she asked, clutching her chest.

"What?" I asked, shivering in the cold.

"Your top. The top of your bathing suit?"

Suddenly it hit me. Dottie had the misfortunate realization that her new best friend was a *boy* and she screamed as if in some elementary school adaptation of *The Crying Game*.

Stunned, but needing to respond, I quietly murmured, "I'm a boy."

Dottie then grabbed her pansied head and screamed in all her Shirley Feeney glory—at the pansy in front of her with no top.

"She's a *boy!*" Dottie cried, finger pointed towards my bosom.

I've often wondered what ever happened to Dottie. I like to imagine that she did go on to find her own Carmine Ragusa and her white picket fence and 2.5 kids.

I do know I would like to tell her one thing, though. I *have* found my top.

In fact, I've found a lot of them.

2

The Queen of Outer Space

Standing at home plate, I held the heavy wood stick behind my head, ready to strike, as my eight-year-old arms quivered nervously. It was my first time at bat for my team "The Orioles," and my first time before an audience of any kind. I trembled from stage fright but with no apparent stage. Dirt fright.

"You just have butterflies in your stomach!" my mom said.

I had looked for the butterflies in the blueberry muffins I threw up behind the dugout just moments before. She had made the muffins that morning from a powdered Jiffy mix—blueberry muffins with no real blueberries in them. My mom usually made this sugary breakfast treat when something was wrong—when I was sick or when one of my too many hamsters had died. She knew that I would not fare well in baseball my first day and the least she could do was console me with muffins I would most likely throw up along with my butterflies.

The ball came so quickly. Head snapping back from the

impact, my freckled nose stung with the heat of the injury as the baseball hit me square between the eyes. But like most effeminate little boys who know better, my first thought was not the pain, but that I not act like a *girl* in pain. However, it was no use. I've never been very good at hiding my feelings and when one doesn't hide one's feelings, one takes the chance of acting like a fag and when a boy acts like a fag, what that really means is that he acts like a girl because only girls have feelings. The muffled snickers, guffaws, and chortles of other boys' parents filled the air as my eyes watered in stung oblivion.

When I regained my sight, the first thing I saw was my father on the sidelines, alone, looking exasperated and embarrassed. My father wanted to be proud of me as much as I wanted him to be proud of me. He had taught me how to pitch and catch a ball, had ceremoniously delivered to me my first baseball glove. However, the only true reason I was in Tiny League baseball was to please him and we both knew he might as well have thrown the ball that hit me himself. But I loved my father and I knew he loved me. *This was for my own good* both our expressions said.

I walked to first.

The day my dad came home and announced that I would be playing with the Orioles, I was delighted! I had just learned about this North American songbird—known for its musical whistle and beautiful feathers—in science class, and assumed that bird-watching expeditions with my father would provide us with the father/son quality time that I secretly craved.

"No—baseball, for the *team* the Orioles," my father announced.

Stunned and not knowing what to do, I did what most future sports recruits do—burst into tears, ran to my room, and flung myself onto my bunk bed, arm over face, more Ruth than Babe.

In the other room, I heard my mom quietly arguing with my father.

"He's not old enough yet!" she whispered. "He's so little. What if he gets hurt?"

"He *needs* to get roughed up a little. Be around other boys his age."

"He's only eight."

When I was little, I wasn't a Momma's Boy, I was Momma's Toy. My mother adored me, loved me with a kind of unbridled motherly joy I rarely saw in other children's mothers. She had always encouraged my uniqueness and fussed over me endlessly.

"He's not a sissy—he's special!" she would tell admonishing relatives who discovered me wearing my grandmother's summer dress. "He's sensitive and artistic!"

When I was a kid, the actor in me was already apparent. When I wasn't being overly dramatic, I was the family clown. Because I loved make-believe, my favorite holiday as a child wasn't Christmas—it was Halloween.

Each year in my elementary school, which was a trailer in the parking lot of our church, the thirty or so of us students of all grades would show up at school fully outfitted in our Halloween costumes for the day. I loved that first impression, of walking into the trailer as a cat or a mouse or a lion. My mother always made sure that my outfits were the most elaborate. Linda was something of a seamstress when I was little. She made most of our clothes from patterns she would buy at Woolworth and possessed a strong urge to create. She belonged to the era she lived in—the 1970s—and arts and crafts projects of the "Holly Hobby" variety littered our house in various states of completion. She made her own jewelry, fashioned macramé plant holders from rope, and had a particular talent for crafting ceramics, which she painted with metallic pastel colors.

I had decided that for my eighth Halloween, I would dress up as a spaceman at school. Rising to the occasion, my mother worked furiously on my costume for a week. She bought yards of shiny silver metallic fabric and other materials one might find in space.

The night before Halloween, my spaceman suit was not ready. My mom tucked me in and the familiar rat-a-tat-tat of her sewing machine lulled me to sleep. After being up all night, my mother, bleary-eyed, finally presented her masterpiece to me. Standing in front of a full-length mirror, I climbed into the clingy, shiny metallic bodysuit that covered my torso. I slid on even tighter silver tights to cover my little chicken legs.

It was at this point that my Halloween outfit took a tragically wrong turn.

My mother took out a metallic makeup kit and began to make up my face, applying silver eyeshadow, 1970s white lipstick on my lips, and golden blush to my chubby cheeks. And finally, the cherry on me, the sundae—glitter flecked onto my cherubic face.

She took my head and bobby-pinned onto it a sort of Kabuki headdress made out of aluminum foil and cardboard. Two antennas stuck out prominently on either side of my head, made of tampons that my mother had wrapped in foil and taped onto the helmet. She then went to her closet and pulled out a pair of white Nancy Sinatra boots that zipped up the side and put me in them.

Facing the mirror, I didn't see a spaceman. I saw a drag queen.

"Oh look at you! You are adorable! Don't move, I've gotta find the Polaroid!"

Gazing at the silver metallic and glitter-kissed image of myself in the mirror, I knew that I didn't look like a spaceman. But my mother had worked so hard on the costume and I didn't want to burst her bubble. She seemed so happy.

My mother came back and took my picture so that she would have a record of her sparkling masterpiece for posterity. Because of the combination of glitter, aluminum foil, and silver stretch fabric before her, the flashbulb bounced off me so brightly it blinded us both momentarily. My mother had turned me into a seventy-pound light prism. Then it was time to go to school.

It is a little known fact that 1973 Ford Mavericks were not designed for tampon headdresses. Unable to sit upright, I was forced to lie down in the backseat of my mother's car as she drove the twenty minutes to my school. I lay in the back of the car, gazing up at the San Gabriel Valley sky, peering off into distant galaxies, unchartered solar systems that I, the spaceman, would very likely never explore. I imagined it would be very hard to find silver eyeshadow in the far reaches of space.

Arriving at school, my mother helped me out of the car so as not to disturb my outfit. She took one more Polaroid and kissed me good-bye.

"Happy Halloween! Have a great day! And let me know what they say about the costume!" As she drove off I turned towards the school and struggled to walk in the white high-heeled boots that went up to my hips. As I approached the classroom trailer, I noticed my fellow schoolchildren milling about. No one else was in a costume.

Several of the very normally dressed children, upon sighting me, the Space Queen, began to laugh and point their fingers. The morning sun collided with the glitter that covered my face, drawing attention to me like some kind of effeminate klieg light.

Each morning, before we went to class, all thirty students would gather around the flagpole for the Pledge of Allegiance in the parking lot that also housed our trailer school. Each day, a different student would lead the Pledge, standing in front of all the other students, leading the school in our patriotic oath. Posted in the classroom was a list of student names, alphabetized, that detailed the order of who would lead the Pledge of Allegiance each day. I remembered that Shannon Carlton had done it the day before. Oh no. C-A . . .

I "ran" in my high heels to the classroom to look at the list, terrified at what I might find, all the while trying to balance the enormous space helmet on my head.

Miss Barden, our teacher, stepped out of the trailer where she was preparing for the schoolday. Upon seeing me, she tired to repress a gasp.

"Craig, what are you wearing?"

"I'm a spaceman," I murmured.

"Well, you know we aren't celebrating Halloween anymore. It's the devil's holiday. Don't you remember? We talked in class last Friday about how we weren't going to dress up for Halloween anymore?"

"I was home that day! My mom was on *Let's Make a Deal*!"

"Oh dear. That's right."

The previous Friday, I had stayed home from school so that I could watch my mother and my aunt on the game show. My mother dressed up as a baseball player. My aunt was Pocahontas. My mother made both of their costumes and when my aunt actually got to play, winning a stereo/TV console in the process, my mother was convinced that she had gotten the break due to my mother's expert costume design.

But today, no deals were going to be made at Sonrise Christian Academy. I was the next one on the list to lead the school in the Pledge of Allegiance—to lead twenty-nine other children *not* dressed up for the devil's holiday in women's clothes.

"Please, Miss Barden. I can go home and change. Please don't make me lead the Pledge of Allegiance!"

"Now, Craig, it's your turn, honey! There's not enough time for you to go home and change. It's time to salute the flag now! It'll be fine. Is that—glitter?"

Reluctantly, I entered the gathered circle of children that I was to address.

"You look like a total space hooker!" Jesus said as I passed him. God, I hated that boy. Jesus was a fat Mexican boy who hated my guts. To be a bully with the name of Jesus in a Christian school is to know power.

"What planet are you from? Uranus!" inspired even more peals of laughter.

I stood by the flagpole, afraid to turn around and face the teaming mob. When I did face them, several students were blinded by the reflection of the sun off my aluminum-foil headdress.

I looked at Miss Barden. She nodded that I should go ahead.

I gathered myself, but the public humiliation was too great for my eight-year-old coping mechanisms.

"I pledge allegiance to the flag."

"More like 'fag'!" Jesus laughed.

With my hand pressed to my silver-spandexed heart, I

started to cry, as the other students laughed and laughed at the TV-dinner-with-legs standing before them.

". . . Of the . . . ahuhuhuhuh . . . United States of America. And . . . ahhhuuuhh . . . to the nation for he which she stands. . . ."

"*She* stands?! HAHAHA!" Frank laughed.

". . . one nation under God . . . ahhhuuuhhhhh . . . indivisible . . . ahhuuuhhhh . . . for liberty and justice for . . . ahuuuuhhhhh . . . all."

The rest of the morning I suffered through the kind of wrath that we had studied in Bible class. I kept my costume completely intact, knowing that my mother had worked very hard on it for a week. As the day wore on, my headdress slowly began to deteriorate. Small pieces of foil began to shake loose from its patchwork design as I went about my business.

At lunch I sat with the only person brave enough to call me their friend—Brenda Bowden. Brenda Bowden was my best friend. She was my only friend as a child. Her father had grown up with my dad in Silver City, New Mexico—a town that, in this metallic get-up, could have welcomed me as Homecoming Queen.

The other children couldn't take their eyes off me. It was as if they were memorizing every single detail of my outfit for later teasing purposes.

"My hat is falling apart," I said, struggling to keep it together. Brenda offered up her help, trying to fold pieces of loose foil back into the cardboard.

Suddenly, while I was eating the chocolate pudding my mother had packed in my lunchbox, one of my "antennas" lost its aluminum casing entirely, exposing a Tampax tampon taped atop my head. My mother had left the wrapping on the tampon before she encased it in foil. (So she could use it later?)

The other children began laughing uproariously. Neither Brenda nor I understood what had taken them from mild amusement into fits of sidesplitting hilarity, so we ignored them.

The exposed tampon remained on my head for several minutes more, until a particularly strong gust of wind blew it off my headdress and into my pudding. Mortified, I immediately checked the remaining transmitter to make sure that it was still in place. When I reached up, I knocked it off and the entire helmet dissolved into a cascade of foil, Scotch tape, bobby pins, and cardboard.

Later, when my mother picked me up from school, she couldn't wait to hear how my costume had gone over.

"What happened to your space helmet?"

"It fell apart," I said.

"Oh, darn it! I was knew I should have used more tape! Sooooo! . . . What did everyone say? Was it the best costume? Was everyone jealous?!" she asked as we drove away.

"Oh my gosh, everyone *loved* it!" I lied. "They all said you are the best mom ever, to make me a costume like that!"

As we drove down the road, I was glad I had lied to her, even though I knew lying was a sin. She seemed so happy and proud and she had worked so hard on making my Halloween the best it could be.

When my father saw my costume, he hit the roof.

"He's got makeup on!" he observed.

"He's a spaceman!"

"Craig—go take off that makeup."

I went to the bathroom and looked in the mirror. Now that I was alone, I actually thought I looked kinda pretty with lipstick on. I posed in the mirror for a while before taking the washcloth to my face.

A week later, I was at my first Orioles practice. Based on my deplorable ability to either hit or catch a baseball, I was relegated to right field—the least-esteemed position a baseball player can have. I hated baseball. Hated it. I hated the rough-housing boys. I hated my coach. I hated the ball. I did, however, *love* the outfit.

3

The Tao of Poo

There are certain defining experiences that happen in the life of every child, experiences that set the stage for one's life, revealing themes and courses of direction and morals to the story. If the child is lucky, he will realize this at the time. If he isn't particularly perceptive, he might not realize the power of this experience until, say, sitting down to write a book about himself.

But whether or not one realizes it at the time, the psychology is set in motion. The defining experience takes hold and there is no going back. Hopefully this experience will be supervised by an elder, a mentor if you will, who will help the child put the experience into a context from which the child can glean deep meaning. What that elder whispers into your ear will become your motto, your very own bumper sticker as you yourself become an elder and learn to defend yourself in the concrete jungle.

"Hi, I'm Gay!"

It must have been disconcerting for my grandma to see her

once untainted name become the label of a homosexual political movement in the early seventies. Within our family she
wasn't Gay, though. She had, like most parents of children's
parents, been christened with another, less controversial handle by her one and only grandson, me—Nee Naw.

Nee Naw had always been the star of the family. Worldly,
hysterically funny, and dramatic, she was utterly and completely herself. The constant stream of Nee Naw mottoes and
sayings floated in the air like fortune cookies with wings. She
meant what she said. She had lived a full, crazy life and believed that it was all for naught if not for the benefit of passing
on her pearls of wisdom to anyone who was impressionable
and willing to listen.

While I idolized Nee Naw, we rarely spent time together
alone when I was a little boy. I was too starstruck to ever truly
feel comfortable in her presence. But somewhere around the
age of seven, she decided that it would be a good idea if she
and I bonded, so she arranged to take me to the Los Angeles
County Zoo.

I had no idea that this day would crystallize all the themes
to come along in my life. I just knew that I had always loved
caged animals, a predisposition that would replicate itself in
my love life as an adult. My grandma showed up in one of
my favorite outfits of hers—a pale green blouse with white
polka dots and matching pale green stretch pants. Nee Naw
was quite a beauty in her day. Having been married six times
by the age of fifty, she had finally pulled out the white flag
and realized that she wasn't any good at the love thing and
instead resigned herself to the many Harlequin romance nov-
els that surrounded her commode. She had recently survived
a partial mastectomy after doctors found a small lump in one
of her breasts.

"The doc told me the lump was in one of my milk ducts. I told the doctor, I don't have milk ducts, I have milk *duds*. Cut 'em off! I don't need 'em anymore!" And she didn't. For Nee Naw, the most liberating thing that could have ever happened to her as a woman was to stop behaving like one in order to get a man.

Since then, aside from her smart outfits, she had let herself go physically, defiantly. She began to enjoy the role of grannie, having finally laid her sexuality to rest. She gained weight, but as all children know, grandmas are better when pleasingly plump.

On the way to the zoo, my Nee Naw drove like her usual bat out of hell, windows down, wind whipping about us on the 101.

I'm not sure what possessed my grandma to have this sudden burst of grandmaternal altruism. Perhaps she saw that I was becoming a sissy and thought I needed time with a masculine role model. My Nee Naw was far from "the little old lady from Pasadena." She swaggered when she walked, smoked pack after pack of Carlton cigarettes, cursed like a sailor, and had a very serious gambling problem. She had an avid appreciation for off-color jokes and wore cateye glasses beneath an immaculate gray beehive.

As we walked into the gates of the L.A. zoo, it was a particularly smog-fogged afternoon. Nevertheless, my grandma lit up one of her famous Carltons between her fingers. I noticed how glamorous she looked holding it, wrist bent fancily upward. It then occurred to me that she thought smoking made her look more feminine.

"I'm gonna smoke when I grow up," I announced.

"Oh really?" she smirked, looking down at me. "Why wait till then? Here, have one!"

With that, Nee Naw pulled out the Carltons and offered her seven-year-old grandson a smoke. Nervously, I took out the cig. It surprised me how light it was, and for years I thought "light" cigarettes referred to how heavy the cigarette was to hold in one's hand, rather that its content of tar and nicotine.

My grandma pulled out her lighter, which was cased decoratively in vinyl, and lit the fag. After she put me out, she lit the cigarette.

I took a puff and almost immediately felt myself go green with nausea. I retched.

"See! Ain't smoking glamorous?!" she said, coughing along with me. "Now that you know what it's like, I don't wanna *ever* see you smoking a cigarette again as long as I live, got it?"

I nodded as I coughed.

And with that, off we went, gazing at the alligators, lions, and giraffes. While we walked along, I couldn't help but feel bad for the animals in their cages. They seemed so bored. I had always had this sort of supernatural ability to empathize with other creatures. Sometimes it made being alive difficult to handle. As a child I felt the pain of every living thing, even insects. I was known to cry out in mourning even over splattered insects on the windshield of our car during family road trips. With every splat I would become inconsolable.

"Noooooo! Dad, don't drive so fast! Waaah!"

The guts of each crushed bug happily going about it business made me feel as though my family and I were coldblooded murderers hell-bent on destruction.

Members of my family knew that I was going to need toughening up in order to survive in this world, and Nee Naw was the toughest one of all.

The last exhibit on our zoo journey was the chimpanzees. We stood at the exhibit's fence, the sun baking our backs.

"Ha! That one looks just like your aunt Carol!" my grandma laughed. She lit up another Carlton just as several other zoo-goers joined us at the railing separating us from the monkeys' artificial environment.

As I watched the monkeys, I felt that they were just a tad too intelligent for their predicament. They looked incredibly pissed off at having been flown in from the African jungles and confined to a slab of cement painted to resemble a rock.

The chimps looked at us with passive contempt as they all congregated at the highest peak on the rock. Huddled together like a monkey football team, they seemed to be discussing something intensely. They seemed unnaturally focused and united.

Then, as if on cue, they all turned to face their dozen or so human gawkers.

One of them, the largest, who seemed like the leader, reached back and shat in his hand.

"Oh! Well, that is just disgusting!" my grandma moaned. She strained in the afternoon sun to see more, her hand shielding the sun above her eyes.

We then witnessed what was perhaps the singular most successful act of simian civil disobedience ever. All the chimpanzees joined their leader, reached back, and began hurling their monkey shit—in our direction.

Chimpanzee poo rained down from the sky, like some plague of biblical proportions, as men, women, and children quickly ran for cover.

Being that my grandma was too old and out of shape to beat the onslaught on foot, she instead dropped her cigarette, threw me to the ground and covered me with her body as

monkey feces hailed down upon her green-and-polka-dot outfit.

I started crying, muffled by the fat of my grandma's upper
arms.

The monkey grenades seemed to just keep coming. The
sound of crap hitting the ground around us was deafening.
Underneath my grandma, I heard people's filtered screams as
they ran. My Nee Naw, though, was silent, as if she had been
trained in the Grannie Marines for just such an occasion.

And then it was over. Nee Naw, stunned and horror-struck
by what had just played out, surveyed the damage. She stood
up, arms held outwards, like Jesus on the cross, barely able to
move or comprehend her sorry state.

"Goddamn you monkeys!" she screamed. She helped me up
off the ground. I was rather poo-free but when I saw her, I
couldn't believe my eyes. Her entire backside was spotted with
shit. The back of her behive, which was falling apart, was
similarly soiled.

As we stood up, we could barely comprehend this assault
on our senses. I blubbered confusedly as we moved to a
nearby park bench which sat peacefully under a shade-
providing tree. My grandma took out a handkerchief and
began to delicately clean herself off.

"Shit!" she cursed. Then, realizing the irony of that comment, she betrayed herself with a half-giggle. "Damn monkeys."

Her ability to maintain a sense of humor in the face of such
horror calmed me down. My crying softened into a childlike
whine of uncertainty.

As my grandmother cleaned the monkey poop off her,
something happened that, had I not been there, I would not

have believed myself. It was one of those punctuation marks to an experience that life sometimes throws one's way. Sometimes the punctuation is a period. Sometimes it's a question mark. This was an exclamation point. A bird happily grooming itself in the branches of the tree above our park bench relieved itself violently into what was left of my grandma's hair bun. Jerking away from the bench, Nee Naw reached up to confirm what had just happened. Her hand pulled away, covered in the white goo.

This insult, added to the already very messy injury she had just endured, was the final straw. At that point, my Nee Naw had a very scary—but well deserved—nervous breakdown.

"Aaaaaahhhhhheeeeeeeaaaahh!" she screamed, shaking her whole body in an effort to cast off the mounds of animal waste she sported. She shook like a dog attempting to shake off mud.

After that, my grandma did something that made me love and respect her forever. She walked back to the monkey exhibit, where unhappy zoo employees were busily mopping, picked up a handful of the offending feces, and with all of her might threw monkey shit back at the monkeys. This final action caused her beehive to disintegrate completely but she didn't care. She had hit one of the chimps in the face with its own shit and she laughed maniacally as it ran around to the other side of the rock.

Later, after cleaning up in the zoo's shower facilities and threatening lawsuits all the way, my grandma lit another Carlton. As we walked back to the car, she explained an important philosophy of hers to me. The philosophy that I would later adopt as my own.

"I told that monkey! Craig, it's much worse to get hit in

the face with your *own* shit than with someone else's. Remember that."

My grandma taught me not to take shit from anyone, man or monkey. The stage was set. Life, I would later discover, was a zoo with not an umbrella in sight.

Habbada Habbada

Driving me to school one chilly Texan morning, my mother was in an unusually perky mood.

"I hope there's sex in heaven 'cause I sure do like it!" she blurted.

I froze. My mother had never talked about sex, let alone her having sex. The closest we had come to that subject was the year before. I had come home from school and found a book strategically placed on my bed called *Almost Twelve*. I was fifteen.

I could understand why my mother (or anyone) would hope there's sex in heaven but I never knew why my mother had become a born-again Christian in the first place. All I knew was that in the early seventies, we suddenly started living in church. My tattooed, sideburned rocker dad resisted conversion as long as possible. He was the lead singer of a rock and roll band called Whiskey, and since his name is Cecil, he changed it to a more rock-and-roll-ish sounding handle— Ed—during Whiskey's incarnation. I thought the "Ed" dad was totally cool and one of my most defining moments came when Wolfman Jack played Whiskey's one and only single on his radio show. Their song, "You Break My Face," never really went anywhere although it did foreshadow what lay ahead for the lead singer's son.

Eventually, the demands of supporting a family with Ramada Inn "gigs" proved to be too much for Dad. Ed put on a tie, Cecil reemerged, and he allowed himself to get saved. "If you can't beat 'em, join 'em," seemed to be the sheepish expression tattooed on his face for years afterward. Nearly all of my childhood and adolescence revolved around the dramas and machinations of an evangelical, nondenominational, charismatic church in our suburb of Dallas, Carrollton.

We went to church—not only every Sunday morning, but Sunday evenings and Wednesday nights as well. On top of that, my mother was the pastor's secretary and worked five days a week in the church office. When she wasn't typing up the newsletter, she counseled hookers, drug addicts, and baby killers on their "prayer line," the phone number of which was prominently displayed on a billboard downtown that read JESUS IS COMING! Our smiling, bespectacled Pastor Joe's face filled the advertisement, sporting hair styled by Fix-a-Flat.

Our modest church consisted of about a hundred disenfranchised loonies and their poor unsuspecting offspring. Like all microcosms of society, there were cool people and uncool people. A church service never went by without someone standing up in the middle of the sermon and, hands raised to the roof, bursting into a nonsensical, tearful spiritual spasm we called "speaking in tongues." The people who spoke in tongues were cool. Very cool.

No one in my family had ever drawn attention to themselves by speaking in tongues and I was always a little embarrassed. Speaking in tongues was the ultimate status symbol in our world—a glamorous foreign language that my parents couldn't master. A person the Holy Spirit chose to speak through had to be special, at least in God's eyes, which, consequently, made them special in the eyes of all those that looked up to God. And the people in my church looked up to God. They wanted to know what God was reading, what look he was sporting that season, and what his "top ten" list was that year. To us, God was the one and only celebrity worthy of a fan club.

The person who spoke in tongues would all at once stand up in the middle of the sermon and erupt like a dormant volcano, screaming out gibberish that sounded like a Chinaman struggling with Hebrew. Pastor Joe would cautiously listen to the tearful twaddle. Then the "chosen" one would shake violently as if zapped by a heavenly stun gun, arms flailing and face twitching. The person would then collapse spread-armed onto the floor, but only once everyone had cleared the way in anticipation of the grand-mal seizure that was sure to follow—a state of oblivion known as "being slain in the spirit."

The adults had numerous tongue-speakers in their congregation. In youth group, which is where I mostly existed, there was only one candidate for "President of Christ's Fan Club" and his name was Carl. Carl was a portly, persnickety goody-goody who was losing his hair at sixteen. He always wore a bolo tie and shiny polyester vests stretched to the max, since he was as filled with donuts and Big Macs as he was the Holy Spirit.

Carl was the most devout born-again Christian teen in the congregation, perhaps in the entire world. He was a spirit-filled show-off and I was insanely jealous of him. He played the flute at Sunday service, the only other instrument on stage besides the piano, and his impromptu flautist Jesus jam sessions were something to behold. He was Carrollton's very own Pan, a pied piper that ate too many pies. His warblings would fill the chapel while adults wept, wishing their children could be as saintly as Carl, instead of the backsliding losers they actually were. Carl was the model we were all compared to and there wasn't a Sunday youth group that went by that Carl did not speak in tongues.

One night in youth group, while we were all enjoying some festive crucifix-shaped Easter cookies and grape Hi-C, Carl dropped his Dixie cup as the Holy Spirit once again filled his willing yet unsuspecting pubescent body.

"Panna manna ding! Kooka minga foo!" he cried out, cookie sprinkles still dotting his upper lip, his tongue a ghoulish purple. Without Pastor Joe in the room to interpret, Carl's/God's words fell on deaf teen ears, I'm afraid. Our youth counselors, a married couple named Ralph and Renee, had unfortunately not been given the talents to translate Jesus-ese.

"Peeka meeka manna! Shavala babba! La babba dabba ding doe!"

My parents didn't really support the idea of me being friends with "secular" teens, fearing that I would no doubt succumb to the temptations of cigarettes, premarital sex, and animal sacrifice. It worked out fine with me, because I was gay and could use my devotion to Christian chastity as a cloaking device for my utter lack of interest in screwing girls. Looking back now as a gay man, I am shocked at how many queens were there. Church is the best place to hide if you're a closet case because they don't approve of men having premarital sex.

My best and only parent-approved friend in high school was Melissa Wilcox, whose parents were even stricter than mine. Melissa was a friend who, while sitting in a mall showing of *Superman II*, abruptly got up and walked out of the theater. After realizing she was not going to return, I found her in the movie theater lobby patiently waiting for me.

"What's wrong?" I asked. "Are you okay?"

"J.C.," she whispered, her arms folded disapprovingly.

"Penney's? That's not in this mall."

"The cop, when that alien blew up his car, he said—" she mouthed the words "Jesus Christ." "I promised my dad I would leave the theater if someone in the movie took the Lord's name in vain."

Fuck, shit, cunt, pussy—those words were all acceptable to Melissa's dad. Anything that made sex sound as repulsive as it is, was fine. But the moment someone said "Christ" or "Jesus!"—God didn't like that. Apparently, our Heavenly Father doesn't buy into the idea that all press is good press.

Being Melissa's friend wasn't easy, especially since all there really was to do in Texas is go to the mall and see movies. It's hard to find a movie without a "goddamn" in it.

Later, our friendship would be irreparably damaged after my mom talked me into asking her to go steady with me. Melissa and I had never even thought of each other as possible romantic material. But my mom, unable to grasp the idea that a boy and girl could just be friends, talked me into believing that Melissa was patiently waiting for me to sweep her off her feet. I asked her to go steady at a Bennigans and she just started laughing. Afterwards, we went to see *Yentl* and she walked out of the theater midmovie because she thought it promoted lesbianism.

We had become friends after enrolling in a door-to-door missionary program called "Spreadin' It!" Spreadin' It! was an outreach program that went to the homes of poor sinners whose main transgression was coming to our church, filling out an information card, and giving us their home address. We targeted "holiday visitors"—people who had innocently visited our church on Christmas or Easter with no idea that their names and addresses would wind up on a missionary hit list. We were in the business of saving souls, and if that meant building up our financially strapped church with new tithing members every week, well, that wouldn't hurt, either.

There were two branches of Spreadin' It!'s outreach program—an adult unit and a teen unit. I was one of three teenagers in my Texan suburb to take the six-week course that taught us how to save a person for Jesus. The course was highly complicated and required so much memorization that my grades in school suffered. As it was, I wasn't a very good student. My parents didn't really mind much. They were of the belief that this world would all be over any day now because Armageddon was coming.

Thanks to our religion, we spent the most sinful holiday—New Year's Eve—bunkered down in church, away from the boozy, orgiastic devil worship that went on in the homes of normal families.

Every New Year's Eve, Pastor Joe promised that "this was the year the Lord returns," meaning "the Rapture"—the day when Jesus would descend from Heaven on a cloud and we born-again Christians would rise into the sky to meet Him with trumpets blaring in the background. The whole thing would be very Industrial Light and Magic, and sponsored by Pepsi.

Since Pastor Joe had promised that this would happen

every year for fifteen years and it never did, you'd think his credibility would start to wane. Not among our optimistic bunch. We prayed for the end to come—for all those heathens that were enjoying their lives to get their asses kicked but good. I knew The End was coming and I was determined to be ready for it. And I would apologize for my homosexual lusts by saving a few other teenagers via my missionary work in the meantime.

Now, I've always been confused by the whole missionary thing. The Bible clearly says that on the Judgment Day, the saved and the innocents—those who have never heard "the good news"—will instantly be beamed up to Heaven. Why Christians go out of their way to give someone the choice to be saved—when their naiveté would automatically guarantee them a place in Heaven anyway—always dumbfounded me.

Most Christians' main reason to save souls has nothing to do with altruistic concern for the unsaved spirits of beer-swilling hookers or drug addicts. The main reason most of them save souls is because they want an extra room added to their condo in Heaven.

I was no different, except that I never really liked thinking about Heaven. Maybe it's just me, but the idea of living for Jesus one's whole life, just so you can enter another realm where you're awarded the lucky privilege of praising that same deity, day and night, for all of eternity, seems a little like a rip-off to me. Shouldn't the reward for sacrificing your earthly life to Jesus be getting to focus on yourself for a change once you die? But no, it's just a continuation of the Jesus worship you obsessed on your whole mortal life.

In Heaven, there is no sickness, no traffic jams, no getting bumped off AOL, and no episodes of *The View*. You'll get to meet all your favorite celebrities, like Princess Diana and

Marilyn Monroe, and you will finally have something in common with them—unending servitude to God. God created angels as slaves whose sole purpose is to do nothing but praise Him. Now, when people say they want to live a Godlike existence, I just tell them to get some personal assistants.

Then again, no one wants to go to Hell. Hell means excruciating pain and "constant thirst" for eternity—even though you have no physical body or nerve endings to feel pain or thirst.

But I've always had somewhat of an "issue" with the way this concept of life has been structured. With its laws, if you will. It has always bugged me that this "life" is set up in a way, that the more you experience, the faster you die. Fatty French food, martinis, smoking, sex, anything more adventurous than, say, gardening, increases one's chances of croaking. In other words, lead a bland, uneventful life and you'll be rewarded with a healthy, long one.

Of course, this wasn't what I was thinking while going door to door with Melissa on our Spreadin' It! sojourns. Most of the time, I was too busy worrying about remembering my "lines."

Melissa and I had doors slammed in our faces constantly, which was fine by me because I was secretly terrified by the idea of actually saving someone for Jesus. I suffered from terrible stage fright, although the stage was only a carpeted living room.

Our Spreadin' It! opening line began with "Hi, [insert name here]! I like to talk to someone about Jesus at least once a day."

After weeks of rejection, a sixteen-year-old girl known around the schoolyard as "Nest Girl" and "Herpes Legs" let us in. Her name was Tammy, and she had a frizzy blond Afro (the nest) and seemed to always have strange red bumps on her legs (the herpes). She was a known high-school slut.

Melissa and I entered Tammy's sunken living room with mild astonishment—no one had ever actually let us inside their house. We sat down with her on the couch and handed her pamphlets, which she quickly tossed onto the coffee table.

"Do y'all want a beer?" she asked.

I had the feeling she invited us into her house mainly because she was bored and lonely. She seemed the epitome of smutty teenage angst. She was slightly plump in that way most high-school loosy-gooseys are, and she always looked slightly disheveled, as if she had just been fucked. She had the ashen complexion teenagers get when they smoke too much pot.

Melissa and I gracefully declined the beer and I launched into my "testimonial," which I had patterned after a "sample testimony" from the Spreadin' It! literature, with personal touches thrown in.

"Well, Tammy, I like to talk to someone about Jesus at least once a day."

"You already said that," she bitched. She took a swig of beer and sat back on the couch, her legs spread like a truck driver's. I half expected smoke to begin fuming from her well-worn crotch.

"Oh, yes, well, I was saved when I was eight years old. I had spent many an endless night wondering why I was on the earth. What was my purpose here? I looked everywhere for answers but could find none. Not in movies, TV, not in books—"

"What a minute! You were saved when you were eight?" She sat up, pointing to me with her beer bottle. "Damn! What book were you looking in? Colorin' books?"

She started laughing and pulled out a crumpled pack of

Saratoga cigarettes she had been sitting on. She lit one as a rather dingy Persian cat lunged at her, trying to paw the cigarette out of her hand, almost hysterically.

"Fluffy you want another one?" With that she removed another Saratoga and placed it on the couch beside her. The cat began wildly chomping down on the cigarette, her mouth filling quickly with shredded tobacco.

"Anyway, as I was saying, I eventually realized that my way of thinking was not working for me. I had heard the 'good news' from my mother, Linda, who had recently found the Lord. She told me that if I accepted Jesus Christ as my personal Lord and Savior, I would not perish, but have everlasting life."

As Fluffy went into a glassy-eyed nicotine "hole," Tammy began biting her lower lip. I could tell that I had gotten through to her on some level. She seemed full of shame, which is exactly what one needs in order to be saved.

"Tammy, can I ask you a question? . . . If you were to die today, would you go to Heaven—or would you go to Hell?" This was the clincher they taught us in Spreadin' It!—make them afraid of dying.

Tammy's lower lip started trembling. She suddenly jerked her hands to her face, covering her eyes.

"*Hell!*" she blurted. She burst into tears. Her herpes legs buckled and she collapsed into a kneeling position on the shag carpeting, putting her hands over her nest hair as if preparing for a nuclear blast.

Melissa and I looked at each other, not knowing what to do next. Nothing in our training had prepared us for emotional outbursts of this magnitude.

"Hell! Hell!" she wailed, like an Irish widow.

I got down on my knees as she rocked, filled with shame

over her sin-lovin' lifestyle. Her hands covered her face so I spoke to her nest hair instead.

"Now, Tammy, I'm going to lead you in a prayer—"

"Are blow jobs sex?" she cried as she jerked her face to me. Her features were as red as the fiery pit she was certainly doomed to.

"What?" I asked.

"Blow jobs. Are they a sin? 'Cause I don't think they should count!" she pleaded.

"Uh—"

"What in tarnation is goin' on in here!" A large woman, who seemed like an older, fatter version of Tammy hobbled into the living room with a frying pan in one hand and a bag of Funyuns in the other.

"Who are you!?" she demanded.

Melissa and I stood up.

"What are you doin' to my baby!?" she screamed. Tammy was still rocking, counting blow jobs in her head. Her mother threw me off completely. I gave up on saving Tammy and decided to nervously save myself from the frying pan Tammy's mom held over her head like a tomahawk.

"Hi, my name is Jesus and I like to talk about Craig to someone at least once a day!"

Having failed at "Spreadin' It!" I decided to be less formal in my quest for God. I would go to Jesus himself—it was time to speak in tongues.

After praying for several weeks, begging God to give me the gift of holy gab, I decided that this would be it—tonight I would trust in Him that my prayers would be answered and He'd anoint me with His Holy Spirit.

I was to attend a record-burning bonfire after the evening youth group service. We had had a guest speaker address the congregation only a week earlier at an "Awareness Seminar" about the evils of rock and roll. Sitting in the dark we looked, horrified, as various subliminal satanic images imbedded in album covers were projected onto a screen. We saw Anton Lavey, the leader of the Satanic Church, peeking his head out of a window in the album art of *Hotel California*. We were told by the speaker that Stevie Nicks was a witch and that most of her songs were spells that made one surreptitiously drop what they were doing to fervently hail Satan. We listened to backmasking—hidden subliminal messages—by the Beatles and the Electric Light Orchestra as our spines tingled. We were also told non-satanic, pointless music-industry gossip that our guest speaker had obviously read in trash like *The Enquirer* as opposed to seen firsthand—rumors that Linda Rondstadt was a cocaine user and that Deborah Harry was a heroin user. For all of us in Texas, it didn't matter that all of this gossip was unfounded, we took it as the gospel truth, evidence of what we had suspected all along about rock and roll and celebrities. We thanked our lucky stars that we weren't in the Satan-ruled cities of Los Angeles or New York, but Carrollton, Texas—a town that wasn't as high on Satan's list of priorities.

After squeezing into my green-threaded Sergio Valente jeans and grabbing my coveted Members Only jacket, I carefully went through my and my sister's record collection to find stuff to toast.

Records in tow, I headed to church and after much ceremony, melted *The Best of ELO*, Blondie's *Parallel Lines*, and the soundtrack of *Saturday Night Fever*. The bonfire was immense. Carl brought a trunkfull of record albums that made my three seem piddly. He announced that he had scoured his own record collection but could find nothing but Jesus-approved gospel, so he rummaged through his neighbors' and distant relatives' turntables from Hell. It didn't matter; I was going to show him tonight. I was going to speak in tongues. God wouldn't let me down.

Everyone surrounded the noxious bonfire and prayed quietly among themselves as they tossed Barry Manilow, Journey, and Air Supply onto the soft-rock inferno. On my knees, I tried with all my might to open up to the flood of Jesus blather certain to follow. Nothing was happening. But I didn't give up. Rocking back and forth like a saintly oil drill, my struggle was immense. Everyone could see something was up with me.

Renee and Ralph came over to me and placed their hands on my head and shoulders, praying for God to enter my body. The other teens followed suit and before I knew it, I was covered in hands. Suddenly everyone liked me and I was finally ready to take my rightful place in the church as God's chosen teen away from pew-chewing Carl. The only problem was—nothing was happening.

After an hour and a half of rocking back and forth and the occasional moan croaking past my lips, I started to sense that everyone was tiring. I began to realize that I was being gypped, God wasn't going to come through me that night, and so, being the people-pleaser that I am, I faked it. Badly.

"Haaaaa! Haaaaab!" I groaned, as if constipated.

Now, you might think that speaking in tongues is easy to fake. It's not. It's really hard.

"Haaaaabada!" Oh, that sounds good; I'll run with this. I could feel all eyes on me in anticipation of what would follow.

"Habbada habbada habbada!" I said. I took a pause to think

of another Hebrew/Chinese-sounding word, but was at a loss. I was drawing a blank, for improvisation has never been my strong suit.

"Habbada habbada hayna! Habbada heena! Habbada ho!"

I had my eyes closed and my hands stretched to Heaven. I could feel the bonfire on my face. Finally, after I ran through every variation of "habbada" I could think of, I opened my eyes and looked at the stony faces before me. It was obvious. They could tell I had faked it and their arms were crossed in knowing disapproval.

Sharon, Pastor Joe's goody-goody daughter simply looked at me, arched her eyebrows, and said snottily, "Habbada?"

Apparently "Habbada" is Godspeak for "I am a total fraud" and, like "oui" in French, it is the one foreign-language word everyone knows the meaning of.

"Paka meena shoo show! Paka show!"

Everyone turned. On the other side of the bonfire, Carl had burst into his expertly believable tongue-speaking.

"Kama la baba! Kama la baba mo mo!"

Everyone ran over to him to get a dose of the real thing—shooting me looks of "thank God, *someone* knows what they're doing around here" as they moved to the other side of the burning Adult Contemporary Rock.

The next week at youth group I was a pariah. A Judas. My former friend Melissa had been the last one to leave the bonfire the week before.

"I saw demons in the flames," she confessed to the group. "They were dancing and stuff." With that, Melissa entered the pantheon of Jesus-endorsed chosen ones that I so longed to inhabit. No, she couldn't speak in tongues—but she saw demons in the flames.

Demons were big that year.

A few months earlier, before I fell out of graces with my church friends for being the religious equivalent of Milli Vanilli, we were all sitting peacefully in the room off the main chapel where we held youth group. Suddenly we heard a loud commotion and hysterical screaming coming from the chapel. Everyone ran into the main area of the church, where the packed evening service was taking place.

Up front, near the podium, seven or so men were lying on top of a struggling man. Pastor Joe was visibly shaken and people were screaming and coughing. Apparently a newcomer to the church had stood up in the middle of the congregation during the sermon, called Pastor Joe a "cocksucker" and after climbing over the shocked rows of worshipers, made a fully committed lunge at him. It was immediately deduced by all that he was possessed of a demon and an emergency exorcism had been called into order.

Everyone gathered around the man, performing spiritual CPR. He shouted cuss words, called the pastor's wife Beulah a "cunt," and was pretty much a potty-mouthed handful. But what was even more terrifying was the mass pandemonium that emerged from the usually composed suburban housewives in the audience. Insanity, madness, and turbulent emotions rained down.

One overweight frizzy-haired woman, whom everyone knew to be a spiritual show-off of the Carl variety, ran up and down the aisles, flapping her arms like a bird. The way things were going that night, I half expected her to take off and fly south for the winter. She screamed, cried out to God, pointing at the possessed man, then came up to me, puked on my coveted Members Only jacket, and fainted into a blubbery, blubbering heap on the floor. I was mortified. That was it. It's hard not to take someone barfing on you personally. Sure, this guy has possessed by the devil, but no demon is worth sacrificing fashion over.

Joe talked to the demon. We found out that the possessed man had been into witchcraft and even had the ability, he said, of moving cars with his mind.

" 'The body of Christ compels you!' " everyone chanted, obviously the only phrase they could remember from *The Exorcist*. The frizzy-haired lady spoke in tongues and rubbed her hands all up and down her plump body as if she had little satanic ants in her pants. The helmet-haired, Kmart–clad women of the congregation even took their shoes off—an act that told Satan they meant business and that the demon was in for some pantyhosed ass-kicking.

Terrified, I went to the church office and called my mom, begging her to come and save me from what seemed like a joint production of *One Flew over the Cuckoo's Nest* and *Godspell*.

My mom comforted me over the church phone.

"Oh, honey, it's okay. It's just an exorcism."

My dad came and picked me up. The majority of the church stayed and chanted until everyone—and the demon— got tired. Carl was one of the last to leave. I'll give him one thing—that boy had stamina. Years later I saw him in a Dallas bathhouse, getting gangbanged bareback by four musclemen, a poppers bottle shoved up his nose, using his flute playing abilities on something other than a flute—yet again the center of attention.

Donuts Not Found at the Craft Service Table

My family moved to Texas when I was twelve. We had become born-again Christians in Southern California, which is fine, but if you truly want to surround yourself with like-minded Christian folk, you need to move to someplace like Texas, where everyone is religious and if they aren't super-religious they are at least God-fearing.

Up to this point, I had been educated at Sonrise Academy—the "Academy" of which was a singular doublewide trailer in the parking lot of my family's church—a magical trailer where I had been sheltered from all the unpleasantness of the real world.

I had always felt lucky to be away from the unforgiving secular realities that most mortal children endured. Nearly every day I would hear my father report on news of other, less fortunate Southern Californian schoolchildren who put their lives in jeopardy simply by attending public-learning institutions.

"A kid was stabbed in a public school today! Saw it on TV."

My mother would shake her head, indicating "what's this world coming to" as she looked at my sister and I wistfully, her eyes glassing in horror as she imagined sharp objects going in and out of our little bodies in some school downtown.

The next day more news would arrive.

"Did you hear? Fourteen. Doused in gasoline and set ablaze right there in P.E. class!"

"Public school?" my mom would ask, although we all knew the answer. If you listened to my folks, public schools were where you sent your child to die a gruesome and horrible death, where Satan was school principal and Charles Manson a substitute teacher.

Upon relocation away from the child-on-child violence which comprised Los Angeles of the early mid seventies, my parents, after much deliberation, decided that it would be fine for me to enter the public education system after we settled. Texas was different. Public schools were safer in Texas. There were fewer news stories about being murdered in public schools there. In Texas, Jesus and his ways permeated people, places, and things. Little Craig would be going from a trailer "school" in a church parking lot to a massive gulag of thousands, yet my parents felt I was strong enough in "the Lord" to handle it. The fact that our new place of worship in Texas had no school in its parking lot also figured prominently into my parents' decision for me going public.

By this point in my life, I had developed no interests in anything whatsoever, having never imagined I would live past the ripe old age of twelve due to incessant talk of Armageddon—the end of the world as predicted in the Bible. Every day of my childhood, I woke up and sat in my trailer school waiting, wondering, would today be the day the trumpets would blare? My family and their friends would talk almost lustily about the dramatic "end times" we were in the midst of. For a child who was developing dreams of a life of his own, there was a real sense of "why bother? It's all gonna be over soon, anyway."

Concerned for the well-being of myself and my family, indeed for all mankind, I broached the subject on the way to orientation at my new Texan public school.

"What are we gonna do the day the world ends?" I asked my mom. I was an inquisitive kid, and my mother had an answer for everything.

"Well, I don't know about you, but I'm gonna get a bucket of fried chicken, sit up on the roof, and watch!" she said cheerfully as she parked our car.

I didn't have it in my heart to suggest that most Kentucky Fried Chickens in town might be abandoned by their minimum-waged employees as the world came to a dramatic end, so I just nodded. I also wondered what exactly we would be watching up on the roof as it all ended. A mushroom cloud? The heel of a boot coming down and squishing us? But I knew when to stop asking questions too. Details such as these didn't seem as important as where to get a last-minute bucket of extra crispy.

We entered the enormous institution of public learning. It was cavernous—much bigger than a trailer. After standing in line for the A–F's we finally got to a desk that revealed a southern fried administrative lady with cateye glasses who asked me what electives I wanted to take that year.

My mother and I stared at the woman blankly. She blinked back at us.

"I'm sorry, what do you mean exactly?" my mom asked in her sweet lilt.

"What are his interests," the bespectacled public school lady questioned, "his hobbies?"

I had none. The world was going to end. Why bother?

"Well, he likes TV. He appeared on TV once—*The One Way Game.*"

My mother explained that just two years earlier, I had appeared on a Los Angeles UHF game show where children were tested on their knowledge of the Bible. The grand prize was, naturally, a Bible, and the respect of people who read Bibles.

I didn't win, having lost stupidly due to a lack of knowledge on Deuteronomy, but seeing myself on UHF channel 39 had a profound effect on me. I liked seeing myself on TV and secretly wished for more of that very thing.

The cat-eyed lady seemed perplexed by this information.

"Well, what do you mean? Drama?" she asked in the accent of her native Texas. "We don't have any extracurricular courses in game shows or Bible study game shows."

And that was how I became an actor—for lack of an interest in anything else. I enrolled in Introduction to Drama.

The night before I started classes, the transition from aluminum siding to brick-and-mortar weighed heavily on my mind. On what can only be attributed to a combination of poor diet and even poorer stress management, I was up all night, pained with gut-ripping bloat. My father worked for Nestlé Foods at the time, and an occupational hazard of his line of work was that I would eat boxes of chocolate bars in one sitting. Nestlé flowed with boxes of free samples. KitKat and Nestlé's Crunch wrappers littered my room night after night as I fed my hungry nerves and thirsty pimples. I cursed the gods for taking me away from the safe womb of my previous school of thirty other kids. Then I remembered that I had been taught there was only *one* God to curse. I didn't dare curse the one and only God, all too aware that a committee of gods was easier to bring a problem to—more democratic, perhaps, than the dictatorship that made up the current administration. Without the courage to curse the singular God, I instead cursed myself.

I entered the school building doubled over in pain, the walls of my lower intestine lined with the sweet confection of my father's employ. Having had no sleep due to these cocoa cramps, I slowly made my way to my very first class, Introduction to Drama.

I squinted as I entered the sterile, artificially lit environment that would serve as fertile ground for budding thespian endeavors. I noticed that almost all the chairs were filled with girls. One spot was available at a large table and, holding my pooching underbelly, I sat down.

Seated next to me were Heather Cox and Cindy Larue, both of whom, I would later discover, were something called "cheerleaders." I would find out that these cheerleaders ruled public schools with absolute supremacy. They had the power to decide who would live and who would die.

While waiting for the class to begin, Heather and Cindy teased their 1978 hair, gazing at their beauty in hand mirrors. They were thirteen but looked thirty. Being that this was my first encounter with public school children outside my church trailer, I decided to introduce myself, but was silenced by a particularly sharp pain in my abdomen. Frustrated by an inability to break wind, I decided instead to break the ice.

"I had really bad gas last night." I grimaced conspiratorially at the unsuspecting beauties, as the sound of a creaking door emanated from my belly.

Cindy and Heather could not believe their good fortune!

Here they were, smack dab in the presence of the very kind of naive halfwit they had always wished for, prayed for, but wondered if really existed. They exchanged a knowing look. Could he be "the one"? A momentary vacuum of disbelief sucked the air from around our table. Then suddenly, in unison, Cindy and Heather inhaled and broke into a screech of laughter as a trapdoor opened beneath me and I slid down a portal to a special hell for socially unskilled, constipated, Christian gay children. This was the confirmation of my worst fears that public school just meant public humiliation.

Why are they laughing? I wondered to myself. I was just being honest, as I *did* have bad gas last night. I had told my mother earlier that morning of my bad gas. She didn't think it was very funny—in fact, quite the opposite. That I was in pain made her love me even more. I had wrongly assumed one's human imperfections would endear one to humans other than one's mom.

Moments later, the laughter and finger-pointing were silenced by a formidable, sixty-something woman sporting a black Dorothy Hamill "do" and too tight pants. The manlady announced her name as Ms. Newrath and that she was to be our drama teacher. I had never seen a presence quite like her before. Mae Newrath licked her chops when she saw me, for she had an insatiable appetite for weak people and happened to be very, very hungry that day.

Drama was to my school what football was to most others—a source of pride. Since our football team, never, not once, won a game, the feverish attention usually awarded that sport was poured into another kind of NFL—the National Forensic League.

The NFL hosted many wonderful and exciting "drama tournaments" in which children from all the other towns in

Texas could come together over a weekend of fierce acting competitions in the pursuit of "trophies." In the land of grown-up acting, this process is called "auditioning"—yet no adult actor would dare endure the two days of heartbreaking competitiveness we poor teens agreed to.

I started off a woefully bad actor. Stymied by the kind of nervous disposition usually reserved for Chihuahuas with thyroid deficiencies, I suffered greatly in my attempts to perform. Worse yet, I received virtually no tutorship from my acting tutor. I never made it out of the preliminary round at Mae's beloved drama tournaments until my senior year. Mae was most passionate about one thing—winning. The tourney awards, cups, and plaques adorned not the mantels of the teen actors who won them but a trophy display case at school. Since I could not act and would never win an award, Ms. Newrath barely noticed me.

However, I wanted to be an actor more than anything. I wanted desperately to perform, to become someone else, anyone but myself. I didn't like myself much but my saving grace in life has been that I *dislike* others more.

An unwavering perfectionist, Ms. Newrath demanded only the best from her pupils. She fancied herself Jean Brodie in her prime—only the crème de la crème would do for her and, unfortunately, my acting smacked of non-dairy creamer.

Aside from deplorable acting abilities and looks, I had other attributes that worked against me in my quest for acting training—my gender. All of Ms. Newrath's favorite students were girls, and she used her pets to make the rest of us actors feel like strays. Because of this, the lineup of productions was decidedly female-centric: *Hello Dolly*, *Annie Get Your Gun*, and *The Sound of Music* were lavishly produced in spite of the many role-starved drama boys.

Due to the lack of any good male roles, the only training ground in those early years was performing at those out-of-town drama tournaments. Within these competitions, there were several categories one could enter with aims of placing with a trophy. Dramatic or Humorous Interpretation consisted of a ten-minute acting scene taken from a popular play or musical in which one stood, alone, and acted all the different parts within the scene—male and female—in a schizophrenic process of acting with oneself. To any self-respecting honey-baked ham this process was sheer hog heaven. The other, less flashy category was Prose and Poetry, in which a pupil would read ten minutes of a story or poems from a black notebook. Prose and Poetry was the training ground for the more esteemed Dramatic or Humorous Interp.

I had been advised by the barely interested Mae to tackle prose and she sent me off to find material suitable for my highly questionable talents. Being the child of a born-again Christian family, my choices were limited.

"Why don't you read something from Deuteronomy? I know you need practice with that one," my mother suggested while scouring the instructions of a new contraption she had just bought—something called a microwave oven. "Or read the story of Jonah and the whale! That one's really dramatic and you could act both parts!"

When I informed her that the Prose piece must be fiction, she reminded me that indeed the Bible would be inappropriate since it was complete fact.

Finally I found a book that I was certain would not offend my parents, that I had loved as a child and was convinced would garner me a Prose Interpretation first-place trophy.

Ms. Newrath approached me and asked what I had chosen to read at my first drama tournament the following weekend.

"Horton Hears a Who," I proclaimed. "By Dr. Seuss."

Upon hearing of my choice, Ms. Newrath took off her glasses and rubbed her weary eyes.

"Of all the great works of literature in the world—Rita Mae Brown, Alice Walker, Gertrude Stein—you pick Dr. Suess? Any other choices?"

"Willy Wonka and the Chocolate Factory?"

While waiting for the judge to show up to begin the competition, I sat patiently in my blue polyester suit on the gym's wooden bleachers. One of the other six teenagers in this soon-to-be contest approached, looking for a place to sit down.

I politely scooted down the wooden bench to make room for my fellow competitor when, suddenly, I felt a stinging shock of pain in my buttocks. Realizing that something was seriously wrong, I jumped up, only to realize that my polyester blue pants had a small tear in the seat.

Rushing to the men's room for a closer look, I discovered that I had been impaled with a toothpick-sized splinter in my rump from the rickety timbered bench.

Unable to see my ass clearly in the bathroom stall, I wanted to get a closer look in the mirror above the bathroom sinks. Scoping out the situation, I saw that the bathroom was quite empty and I exited the safety of the stall.

Quickly moving to the sinks, I fully exposed my buttocks and tried, precariously, to see my wounded bum in the bathroom mirror. Straining and stretching to survey the damage, I realized that the wound was deep. I reached back to try and carefully remove the sliver, when, as if on cue, an older gentleman walked into the men's room, only to find me, spread-cheeked, fully exposed, as if in a state of wanton teen desire.

The color in the man's face left him. He had suspected such things at drama tournaments, such abominations, and spun on his heels for a hasty retreat.

Shocked and embarrassed, I pulled up my pants as the man fled. Realizing that time was running out before my competition began, and unable to remove the damned splinter, I was forced to accept the splinter as part of my person and go on with the show.

Rushing back to the gymnasium, I realized that all the other students were already inside. I was first up in my round and immediately approached the front of the room.

Opening my black notebook, I addressed the crowd. Beads of sweat collected on my forehead from the stinging pain in my rear, not to mention my nerves.

"*Horton Hears a Who.* By Dr. Seuss," I began.

Then, as I surveyed the audience, I noticed that my judge seemed shockingly familiar. I felt the blood leave my head as I identified the judge as the man who had stumbled upon my spread butt cheeks. An expression that suggested the stench of a foul odor consumed the judge's face, complete with pinched up nose and fully pursed mouth. Remembering that the show must go on, I performed Horton and his Who companions quite poorly. The pain, the humiliation in the bathroom prior was just too much for a thirteen-year-old impaled performer to endure, and I placed last in my round—a placement I knew had less to do with poor acting abilities and more to do with a misperception that I had offered my ass to the judge in a desperate, failed attempt at the casting couch.

Act II

In 1981, a magical movie named *E.T.* hit the screens of North Texas. Ms. Newrath liked *E.T.* and decided to stage a tribute to the lovable alien by mounting a review of skits called *E.R.A.*, or *Extra Remarkable Alien.* In this Carrollton take on *The Carol Burnett Show*, I was awarded my first role ever on-stage—of a dying dog in a spoof of a "Chuck Wagon" commercial.

Playing opposite me on stage, as my Ranch Hand master, was the first flamboyantly homosexual male I had ever met—Paco Butte (pronounced BYOOTE, although not behind his back).

Paco had become something of a local Carrollton legend. Flamboyantly "out" at the tender age of fifteen, he wore lavender jeans, sported ascots of every conceivable color, and wore a beret covered with little buttons that decreed slogans such as "It Takes Balls to Be a Fairy" and "I Can't Even Think Straight!" Slightly plump, with bad acne and a slight lisp, Paco was Hispanic and had a rather thick accent he was working hard to lose by watching old Hollywood movies. Imagine Bette Davis on a Mexican soap opera and you have the "fabulouth" Paco.

My empathetic connection to Paco was entirely unreciprocated, as he could not be less uninterested in getting to know me. For Paco, acting was "just busineth."

At the first rehearsal for *E.R.A.* Paco showed up in all his homosexual grandeur. Smoking a pink cigarette, he approached sheepish me.

"So, you're my dog?" he wondered. He attempted a French inhale—very poorly—and instead wound up watering his eyes and snorting his own secondhand smoke, very unglamorously.

"Yes," I squeaked, noticing a button on Paco's "rehearsal outfit," which read, "One in Every Ten Jesuses Is a Mary."

"I see! How nice for you!" he said in his best Bette Davis voice.

Paco slowly moved to the corner of the theater and picked up what looked like a little inflatable donut. He then hobbled back. Something seemed wrong with the way Paco walked— as if he had pulled some kind of muscle. Then he approached a chair, put the donut down, and gently, oh so gently, rested his rather ample posterior atop it.

"Are you okay?" I asked politely.

"Yes, well, I suppose so. I just had a little *emergency surgery* last weekend. The pillow is for purely medical reasons, I assure you. The show must go on, as they say!" Paco said as he clapped his hands together theatrically as punctuation.

I wondered for days about the mysterious donut pillow. It seemed an odd accessory for someone. It wasn't until later in the week, during drama class, that I overheard the true nature of Paco's donut.

Cindy LaRue revealed Paco's not-so-secret secret to Heather Cox as I eavesdropped.

"He was out at the gay bars this weekend. This old guy— like thirty—totally picks him up. They go back to a La Quinta motel and the old guy sticks his wiener up Paco's butt with no lube and rips him a new asshole. He had to go to the emergency room and get stitches. Now he has to sit on that donut for weeks till his butthole heals."

Cindy's tone wasn't judgmental, not even disapproving really—she reported the news of Paco's ripped anus like a professional. She even knew the medical term for what ailed Paco—"anal fissure."

I had never heard of such things. I wondered what that must be like—to be fifteen and having an older man rip one's butthole in a motel. The splinter in my bottom had been painful enough. But a penis, at lease one hopes, is much larger than a splinter. The sheer horror of that image frightened me deeply. I had always been told that gays did such things. Now I saw that it was true. Paco Butte had ripped his butt. The act of sodomy wasn't just unnatural—it required serious medical attention to boot.

Paco carried his donut around school with him proudly, making the grand gesture of drawing attention to his fissure in all of his classes. Paco saw his donut differently from the others—to him it was a badge of honor. He got fucked in a motel with a hot guy and they hadn't. He was unashamed of who he was—my first gay "real" model. And by observing him being himself, something inside of me began to quietly liberate.

After school, my father picked me up as usual.

"How was school, padner?" he asked.

"Fine."

"Tonight we're going to Wednesday services early. There's a memorial for LoRee MacGee and you're mom wants to get a good seat."

LoRee MacGee, a woman as godly as she was boxy, had recently passed onto the other side after being accidentally run over in her driveway one fateful morning while teaching her fifteen-year-old dyslexic son how to pull her car into the garage. After his mother's hollering for him to drive the car forward, Robbie MacGee unintentionally slammed on the reverse with full force, rolling over his mother's curlered head and killing her instantly—all before breakfast.

"It truly is a shame about that LoRee, her poor boy's gonna

have to live with that the rest of his—*what the heck!*" my dad yelled abruptly.

Suddenly, our car was nearly sideswiped by the *putt, putt, putt* of what sounded like a lawnmower.

There, on the passenger side of the car, Paco peeled by on his moped, going the top speed his chariot would allow— thirty-five miles per hour. Wearing lavender jeans, a womanly blouse, and flats, his ascot flowed in the breeze behind him as if waving "see ya, suckers!" to all those in his wake.

"Oh my gosh! That Mexican girl's driving like a bat out of heck!" my father marveled, completely mistaking Paco's gender, for obvious reasons.

As Paco passed us, my father and I took him in. There, atop his moped, Paco perched on his inflatable donut, perfectly centered upon it.

"No wonder she's driving like a maniac—her feet can barely reach the pedals. What kind of seat cushion is that?" my dad wondered aloud.

I thought of telling my father of Paco's ripped anus, but something held me back. Somehow I felt that revealing its nature would be self-incriminating. Some concepts are better left unthunk, I thunk.

Ms. Newrath didn't take to Paco's public display of fissure pride very kindly. Paco's in-your-face sexuality was barely tolerated by her and other school employees. Newrath's wrath was quietly felt in her casting decisions. That was where she wielded her powers of disapproval, and Paco's brief "Chuck Wagon" spoof was punishment for his being so precocious.

Yet, while Paco had actual lines of dialogue, my sole character, a dog, did nothing but wheeze loudly and collapse on stage, the joke being that Chuck Wagon had killed the Ranch Hand's beloved companion. Funny stuff.

I took my role very seriously, studying the various and sundry dogs that roamed our neighborhood, because the Chesters were decidedly cat people.

My family had once owned a dog named Fifi, a toy poodle, a sweet, somewhat hapless creature that was perhaps too good for this world. When I was five, I stumbled upon the postpubescent pooch on our front lawn, only to witness her being raped violently by a raging German shepherd. Not knowing what to do, I ran for my father.

My dad came to Fifi's defense, chasing off Germany's second invasion of France in a dramatic display of emotion. A month later, Fifi's belly began to grow. And grow. And grow. Inside Fifi was the love child of a dog twenty times her size.

Fifi's stomach grew to massive proportions. Eventually unable to move due to her protruding womb, Fifi would lie on the kitchen floor, legs stretched apart, sometimes skyward, by her enormous belly. My mother took to feeding Fifi by hand, a time-consuming effort, and occasionally would be seen carrying the beach ball with legs outside where Fifi could lie on her side and do her business on the lawn. Unable to grasp the concept of pregnancy at the tender age of five, my parents simply told me that Fifi had accidentally sat on a tack. The tack had caused her to get a nasty infection inside of her belly and this was the reason that she was turning into a throw pillow with curly hair and protruding legs.

Eventually Fifi's short life ended, her tiny toy body unable to contain the beast within any longer. Something about her ribs breaking and her heart stopping. The violent demise of Fifi settled it. The Chesters decided to never again own a dog. All species of cats are the same size.

But Fifi's death was not in vain. I drew upon her faint memory for my dying dog soliloquy in *E.R.A.* I died on stage beautifully and the laughter I received during my grand mal seizure was music to my floppy ears.

During the short run of *E.R.A.*, one of the cast members, a girl named Mary, announced backstage that her father had seen our cutting-edge and timely take on *E.T.* and wanted to book the *E.R.A.* troupe into a professional milieu. Her father worked as an events planner and had been hired by a local TV channel's evening news affiliate to supervise the network's Christmas party at the esteemed Four Seasons hotel downtown. *E.R.A.* would be the sole form of entertainment at this unbearably glamorous event. Not only that, but the cast would be performing for the very TV anchors we watched every night. The *E.R.A.* players were overjoyed and intimidated at this taste of "the big time" and Ms. Newrath had no objections to "letting her kids spread their wings." Finally, I had come full circle—the newscasters had warned my parents about the dangers of public school. Now, thanks to my enrollment in public school, I would be entertaining newscasters.

The day of the Christmas party, the cast of ten students arrived at the Four Seasons, brimming with excitement and nervous exhilaration. I was especially tense. I had performed my dying dog to great acclaim at school, but would that success translate to a more worldly audience of Dallas/Ft. Worth celebrities?

When we arrived at the large banquet hall that would serve as our theater, the Christmas party was in full swing.

I entered the large dining hall and immediately spotted my hero—Rowena Krokidas. Rowena Krokidas was the Barbara Walters of local Dallas news anchors. She entered my living room every night, giving me and my family much-needed information on how dangerous everything in the world was.

Seated next to Rowena was her news anchor co-star, Duncan Pitt. The weatherman, Steve, was there. Chad the sportscaster, too. The rest of the hundred or so other local news employees filled the ballroom but something was amiss.

Devoid of a legitimate stage, the cast would be bringing our unique comic stylings to a cleared-off area of the floor in the center of the banquet room. Making my way to the playing area, I heard what sounded like a large belch from behind me. The belch was so loud, I almost wondered if someone had vomited.

Turning around, I discerned that the belch had indeed come from Rowena Krokidas. Several of her co-anchors laughed uproariously at her boisterous burp. On closer examination, I noticed that Rowena's eyes were slightly crossed in an inebriated fashion.

It was only when a man across the room collapsed face first that the *E.R.A.* players and I realized what was happening. Everyone in the room, from Rowena to the cameramen to the grips, was drunk beyond human comprehension. People were laughing, screaming, hooting and hollering from one end of the banquet hall to the other.

Mary's father approached us nervously and wished us a good show and we did what we always did before every performance—said the Lord's Prayer. Holding hands in a prayer circle, several cast members struggled to keep their eyes reverently closed as a beer bottle landed smack-dab in the middle of our circle, spinning like a firecracker as it sprayed our thespian ankles with the fizzy, exploding beverage. I wanted nothing more than to leave my eyes closed for the rest of the evening.

After the prayer, Mary's father demonstrated amazing powers of denial in the face of the rowdy and unruly news people employing him and ordered that "the show must go on." Off he went, leaving us to fend for ourselves.

Paco fired up a shiny colored cigarette in preparation for battle.

"Everyone here is lit!" he said in his best Bette Davis voice. "Jesus Christ, what a bunch of breeders! And look at Duncan Pitt! 'Drunken Shit'!"

First up was a skit that lampooned the character of E.T. Playing the title role, as E.R.A., was Olivia Beatrice. In a bold move against type, Olivia had been cast as the emaciated yet wide-eyed alien for reasons none of the other cast members could quite understand. As rotundly obese as E.T. had been thin, one thing was certain—the spaceship that this Extra Remarkable Alien hailed from carried high-fat, high-carbohydrate provisions.

The plump Olivia entered the playing area and went into character as the adorable E.R.A.

"Phone hooooooooome!" she croaked in her nasally E.T.-like voice.

Soon it was apparent to all that taking center stage with this crowd was akin to having a bull's-eye painted on one's face.

"Hey fatty! HAHAHAHA!" someone from the banquette tables shouted.

Olivia, a naive fifteen, remembered what Mae had taught her. *The show must go on!* she reminded herself, and chose to immerse herself in her character. It is common knowledge that the Christlike E.T. was misunderstood and persecuted by the human race. E.R.A. also laid claim to misfit status and Olivia used the fat-phobic crowd as actorly motivation.

"Show us your tits! HAHAHA!" another patron begged as the drunken journalists laughed and hooted uproariously. Olivia ignored this invitation, knowing that she had enormous boobs. She unconsciously loosened her purple sweatshirt.

Across the room, two drunken TV news employees, caught up in the frenzy, stood and yelled, "You suck!" One of them, a man, laughed.

"Fucking fatty! Eat a ham sandwich, Porky!" the other one, an anorexic woman, cried. The man and the woman then put their glasses down and began making out on the table while others laughed and coughed.

At this point, the other E.R.A. players entered the scene to do a barely audible rendition of "We've Got Magic to Do" from the musical *Pippin*. Paco and I suddenly found our near non-participation in *E.R.A.* to be a godsend. From "the wings," we watched, horrified, as the pernicious crowd hurled food and paper plates while the budding thespians recreated Fosse "jazz hands" choreography in vain. Many of the dancers grimaced back tears.

Paco adjusted his shoulder pads and yanked his terrified canine co-star with him to the "stage."

Paco and I took our places. Another loud belch was heard from Rowena.

"Uh-oh!" someone in the crowd moaned.

"Life on a ranch can make man's best friend hunger for the taste of real juicy beef, padner!" Paco lisped as I assumed my character's position on all fours.

"HA! The tathe of juithy beef!" Duncan Pitt snorted.

Paco bristled but continued.

"Just ask my trusted companion, Spot. I've been feeding Spot here Chuck Wagon for many years now—"

"Look! A couple of flamers!" someone exclaimed. "HA-HAHAHA!"

I looked at the floor, and then began my wheezing act, as

my character Spot began to die. The crowd, instead of taunting me, did something entirely worse by ignoring my death soliloquy altogether, talking loudly amongst themselves. I completed my demise, collapsing to the floor.

Just then, a lone piece of Christmas fruitcake was projected from the mad throng, landing next to Paco just as he made his move to leave the stage. Slipping on the mushy grenade, Paco's legs did something they were quite used to—they went skyward. Landing on his recently ripped backside, he screamed in pain.

I helped my friend Paco up.

"The fruits slipped on the fruitcake!" I heard someone yell. The crowd went wild with laughter as two gay teens stood center stage.

Dogs are loyal creatures. They roam the streets, sniffing for evidence of those resembling them. In that moment, I realized that, like the dog I played, I had found someone like myself in Paco.

I became overwhelmed with emotion—a sense of righteous indignation overcame me, bubbling up from some seemingly inexhaustible and previously untapped source. In that moment, something happened to me that would define my trajectory for the rest of my life.

I stood up for the fruits.

"FUCK YOU, YOU FUCKIN' CUNT EATERS OF SHIT!" I screamed. It was the best I could come up with in that adrenaline-pumped moment. I had never uttered a cuss word before in my life, not even "damn," and half expected to be struck down by lightning right then and there.

The crowd was silenced. It had not occurred to them that one of the teenagers might speak up. Especially the dog. Especially so . . . creatively.

Then, suddenly, all hell broke loose. Rowena rose and immediately stormed Mary's father, who stood by the exit, ready to make a run for it should just such a thing occur.

"Who does that little faggot think he is?" Rowena screamed as her arms flailed about.

Every other member of the ten o'clock news crew rose drunkenly from their seats and stormed Mary's dad. Paco and I joined the other cast members, wisely assuming that there is power in numbers.

Huddling together, we clung to each other like frightened baby seals prepared for an imminent bludgeoning.

Paco grabbed his ascot and, eyeing a nearby fire exit, flipped it over his shoulders and made a break for it. We all followed suit.

While previously appalling in my abilities to perform, from that moment on, my acting talents emerged. Once I had found my voice, I understood the need for art and for speaking up for one's art and oneself in front of insensitive bastards. To me, they were intricately interlinked. I realized that the bad behavior, the misogyny and homophobia of this event wouldn't be on the evening news because the very people who reported the evening news, the media, had caused it. Those in power had a vested interest in keeping things quiet and keeping their bad habits unchecked, I realized.

By my senior year, I had developed fully as an actor, appearing in the starring roles at school. Not only had I moved out of preliminary rounds at drama tournaments, I had actually gone all the way—winning first place trophies in both Dramatic Interpretation and Duet Acting at the state competition. No one had suspected that the quiet, invisible boy named Craig had anything in him quite like this. And I realized that the only thing better than winning in this life is proving people wrong.

6

Why the Long Face?

It has been said that most beautiful babies in the world mature into unattractive grown-ups. I'm not sure who started this rumor but I have found this old wives' tale to be woefully untrue. One look at the adult Brooke Shields and that falsehood is blown to beautiful bits. There are exceptions, of course—Johnny Whitaker, Shirley Temple, and, of course, the unlucky-looking Baby Jane Hudson, among others.

I was a cute baby. No, make that adorable. Better yet, make that delectable. People literally wanted to eat me. My parents would hide all condiments when hungry guests arrived, terrified that their precious baby boy would be doused with Tabasco sauce and swallowed whole like an oyster.

I learned from an early age that cuteness had its advantages. Before I was five, I already knew what my "good side" was in photographs and I worked that right angle for years. Then, around age eleven, the ghastly headaches began.

The doctors didn't know why these headaches racked my tiny little head but believed them to be the logical result of a nasty concussion I had received at the hands of my younger sister Kim.

While happily playing with her dolls one day, Kim had a Vietnam veteran–type flashback of some repressed brotherly cruelty of mine. Dazed and overwhelmed by near total recall of this incident, she fell into a hypnotic remembrance of my crime and decided to take justice into her own six-year-old hands pronto.

Rummaging through my father's trunk of music equipment, she discovered the perfect weapon—a leaden microphone. Carrying the weighty blunt instrument in one hand, her baby doll in the other, Kim searched the house, trancelike, in full vigilante mode. I was quietly watching my favorite show, *The New Zoo Review*, doing something my parents, had they been home, would certainly have reprimanded me for: lying, stomach on the living-room floor, chin propped on palms, with my eyes six inches from the TV.

Upon seeing me, Kim sensed a perfect opportunity. Moving with the all the swiftness and sense of purpose her chubby little legs could muster, she approached me from behind. Overweight for her age, she was not a weak child by any means. Even though she was five years younger than me, Kim always won in our fights, either by sitting on me, body-slamming me, or resorting to the Hiroshima finale of brother/sister wars—farting point-blank in my grimacing face.

The last thing I remember was Freddy the Frog. Freddy was my favorite cast member of *The New Zoo Review* and to this day, I blame him and Speed Racer for making me gay.

I lay facedown on the shag carpet, a lump forming on the top of my head. Kim, feeling pleased with the results, went back to her bedroom where she resumed playing with her many baby dolls, deeply satisfied.

My mother walked into the house, arms full of groceries, to see her only son unconscious on the living-room floor. Dropping the groceries that were the barrier between us, she ran over and chose a most effective tactic to awake me from my stupor—more hitting. I woke up as Rita Moreno screamed, "Hey, you guys!" on *The Electric Company.*

When my headaches began, shortly after my sister's bludgeoning, doctors assumed it was the result of this concussional act of sibling revenge. But something was occurring besides headaches when, for no good reason except for crap genes, my eleven-year-old face began to warp like a vinyl LP left inside a hot car.

At first, the change was subtle. It is not uncommon for a child's face to strain under the influence of budding pubescent hormones. Most children go through a somewhat ugly phase at puberty, a normal burst of pimples and awkward looks. But when my teeth began to turn—to the point of having two front teeth completely sideways—we all knew something was amiss.

My face then began to grow longer, as if melting, elongating into an exaggerated frown. While my lower jaw stretched downward, my upper jaw stopped growing completely at eleven, leaving upper adult teeth nowhere to go but sideways as they struggled to grow.

As the upper and lower jaws tried in vain to formulate a bite, my nose bent—another symptom of a failing infrastructure. My stretched-out face required enormous effort in order to keep my lips together. Imagine a perpetual yawn while trying to keep your mouth shut; this was my daily condition and through this misshapen expression I lived out my entire adolescence.

Eventually my parents had to accept that Craig, their little boy whose epicene beauty had inspired face-pinching and veneration, was turning into a monster before their eyes. By fourteen, I looked like a Picasso sock puppet with pimples.

At sixteen, headaches had become a way of life. It was not possible for me to have a conversation without the *pop-pop-pop*ping of my dysfunctional and strained jaw sockets. Eating was also a loud and laborious demonstration of human sound effects.

Constantly teased and mocked, I had learned to walk the halls of school facedown, staring at my shoes, bearing in mind that at any moment I could look up and surprise an unsuspecting and previously unexposed pupil to the horror of my mug.

Gay, painfully shy, socially retarded; there already had been obstacles to overcome before deformity. As my face melted, the only features that remained unscathed by my misshapenness were my eyes. Through those blinking receptacles, all of teen man's inhumanity to teen man would be recorded for posterity.

"Frankenstein!"

"Gila monster!"

"Ostrich face!"

My dreams of being an actor began to dissolve with every glance in the mirror. The loss of that dream was devastating, for I had only one desire in life—to be a serious actor. Instead, nightmarish visions began creeping into my deformed head: of skipping through Disneyland obscured as Mickey Mouse, of playing "The Creature" in low-budget horror movies.

Around fifteen, it was decided that I should get braces. It was now an established fact that I would be an ugly person in my life and I had begun to accept the face I inhabited as my own. While we could do nothing about my long features, the least we could do was fix those crooked teeth.

While sitting in the examination chair of my soon-to-be orthodontist, Dr. Dougherty, I was excited. In my mind, anything he could do to help my hideous appearance would be a godsend. After examining my mouth, he grabbed my face and asked me to open and close.

Pop, pop, pop.

As usual, the popping gave birth to a headache. As I winced, Dr. Dougherty called my mother over.

"We are going to have to send him to a specialist. There's something seriously wrong with his bone structure and his jaw sockets. I know an excellent maxillofacial specialist," he said.

"Well, okay. But I don't see how getting a facial is gonna help what's wrong with him," my mom replied.

Not quite knowing what to make of this, my mother took me to see the man who would change my life forever—a man whose name seemed the height of irony considering the religiosity pervading my waking world: Dr. Sin.

Within seconds of seeing me, he diagnosed my condition.

"Long-Face Syndrome" is genetic, he told us. The only way to fix it was massive amounts of reconstructive surgery—a painful and grueling process that would require no less than a year of my life. He said it was not classified as cosmetic surgery per se because of my straining jaw sockets. If I didn't have the surgery, it was very likely that my jaw joints would eventually wear out in my thirties—causing a form of lockjaw.

He pulled out "before" and "after" pictures and if my jaw could drop any lower, it would have. There they were—people who looked as ugly as I did, on the left. And on the right—a completely different face bearing little resemblance to the one that preceded it.

I was elated.

"He'll have to wait till he's eighteen to have the surgeries done—when his bones are fully developed," Dr. Sin said.

The three-year wait seemed insurmountable from my teen perspective. I wanted him to put me under the knife right then and there, ripping my mouth out and replacing it with a Farrah Fawcett smile.

Besides the three-year wait, the other obstacle to this magical process of transformative surgery was the cost: thirty thousand dollars. It was not covered by insurance.

My family vacillated between lower and middle class so it was decided that the money issue would be dealt with once I approached eighteen. In the meantime, Dr. Sin told us, I should go ahead with braces as planned.

Almost immediately, my father fell upon hard times financially. He had left his steady job at Nestlé to open his own food-brokerage business, the business was not a success, and hard times just got harder. The prospects of a thirty-thousand-dollar operation began to seem less and less likely, considering our situation.

Meanwhile I had begun to collect *GQ* magazines, looking at all the strong chins, the chiseled cheekbones, barely able to contain my glee that someday soon I would also have a chin that I could sharpen a knife on. But when my father's business began struggling, paying the rent began taking precedence over luxury items like chins and cheekbones.

Knowing that my fate rested on our financial stability to have my face surgery, I began to obsessively monitor my parents' spending. All amenities were a potential barrier to my future.

We Chesters are an empathetic lot. It was not uncommon for a wayward soul to spend Christmas Day with us. Whether it be a divorced middle-aged woman without a family, an elderly woman similarly alone, or a young runaway down on her luck, our home was the land of broken toys, much to my chagrin. And with every customer served, every dollar spent, I saw my hopes and dreams fade.

Unwrapping yet another new shirt Christmas morning, I could contain my repulsion at my parents' generosity no longer. I stood, holding up the shirt as if it were radioactive.

"I don't need a new shirt! I need a new *face*!" I cried, running to my room and slamming the door.

I would have certainly gone nude for those three years if it meant putting that clothing budget towards my future good looks.

After high school graduation, I auditioned for Southern Methodist University's Ivy League theater department. The head of the theater department called my father to tell us I had been accepted into the esteemed program but that he felt I didn't actually need the training they offered. Instead, he felt that I was ready to go straight to New York and start working. There was only one problem.

"That face. It's going to be hard for him with that face," the man said.

Broke, struggling to stay afloat financially, and knowing he could not afford the hefty price tag of the operation, my father called Dr. Sin and said he wanted us to go ahead with the surgery anyway. He told Dr. Sin truthfully that he could not afford it, but would find a way somehow and to bill him for the operation. With that, my father did something that saved my life as sure as if he had thrown himself in front of a speeding train.

A month later I was admitted to St. Paul's Hospital for the first in a series of operations.

The first surgery of the three would require breaking my upper palate, which had stopped growing at twelve, and re-setting it to adult-size proportions. The second and third procedures would be the most dramatic and done simultaneously as Dr. Sin cut, broke and reset my upper and lower jaw into some semblance of a face.

After the first operation, I woke up in the recovery room. The first thing I noticed was that there was no access to the roof of my mouth. Instead of a palate, there was a brace of metal. The taste of blood and metal made me gag. A shiny little key was dangling from my father's fingers.

Every day for a month, the shiny key would be inserted into a small hole in the retainer that occupied the upper half of my mouth. With every turn, my malleable palate would expand, ever so slightly, until a full inch existed between my two front teeth. The device was called an expansion retainer unit and it gave my mouth a six-year evolutionary jump from the twelve-year-old palate I had been left with. Once the gap existed in the roof of my mouth, the teeth were moved into a perfectly straight row, filling the one-inch gap gladly.

Now that the roof of my mouth was as wide as the bottom, it was time for the serious operation to take place.

Being that I would be undergoing a grueling twelve-hour surgery first thing the next morning, Dr. Sin required me to check into St. Paul's Hospital in Dallas the night before.

I imagined what my new face would look like. The greatest and only fear inspired by the surgery was that no one, not even my doctor, knew what the end result would look like until after the surgery and the swelling had reduced. But I didn't care. I could come out looking like the title character in *Creature from the Black Lagoon*, gills and all, and still feel it was an improvement over what I had looking back at me in the mirror.

The next morning, my parents by my side, I was wheeled into the operating room I would spend the next twelve hours in. I moved myself onto the table, fully awake as a nurse injected anesthetic into my arm.

Looking up, I saw my reflection in a lighting fixture. I took a long last look at the face that had betrayed me. *Good riddance.* Like someone in an abusive relationship who has reached their breaking point, I felt no melancholy, no sentimentality at saying good-bye.

As I slipped away, the image of my face grew more and more distant until, eventually, I was gone.

The first thing I saw when I woke up in ICU was our preacher, leaning over me, peering through Coke-bottle horn-rimmed glasses and sporting his usual gray pompadour.

I struggled to speak. Nothing came out.

My mother came into frame.

"Honey, your jaws are wired shut. There's a plastic bite plate in between your teeth so not even air can pass through. You can't talk or eat, but you have a beautiful chin!" She smiled.

After that brief return from the astral plane, I lapsed back into unconsciousness.

I woke up the next day with a sharp shooting pain zipping out the tip of my penis as a nurse pulled on my catheter with glee.

I happen to believe that nurses are much like stewardesses. They are employed to make you feel as comfortable as possible but nearly always wind up doing the opposite. I have formulated this opinion not by unkind prejudice but by a litany of experiences where the medical establishment has failed me miserably. I am of the school of thinking that the customer (or patient) is always right, and I have been known to scream, throw Jell-O, and behave in a most undignified manner in order to get the care I need for myself or loved ones from nurses who behaved like glorified waitresses.

From ICU I was moved to a hospital room, in and out of consciousness and deplorably nauseated from the anesthetic.

Once in my room, I sat up in bed with a start, my mouth watering in anticipation of vomiting. The thought seemed so appealing at that moment, so satisfying. Then I realized that, with my mouth wired shut on a plate, there would be nowhere for it go but right back down.

My mother intuited my state and approached me brandishing wire clippers.

"Do you have to throw up, honey?" she asked as she snipped the wire cutters together in anticipation.

"The doctor showed me how to cut your wires if you need to throw up," she said. "Only thing is, if we snip the wires, you'll have to go back into surgery and have everything reset."

Having no interest whatsoever in repeating the past two days in ICU, I instead focused on the nausea calming pattern of the room's wallpaper—a blueprint of delicate little flowers designed to calm recuperating nerves such as mine.

"You sure you don't need to throw up?" my mom relented, much to my chagrin. It is common knowledge that, when in a state of a potential heave-ho, the last thing you want from those around you is a preoccupation with your queasy predicament.

" 'Cause if you need to throw up, I got the wire cutters right here!" she persisted.

Pretty little flowers. A constellation of sweet little blue pansies. Ahhh. I can do this. I don't have to throw up. Why won't she be quiet?

"You should try not to throw up if you can keep it down. 'Cause if do, you could choke on your own vomit. It'd probably just come right through your nose and then you could suffocate on your puke."

As these words brought me to the brink, I desperately commanded my mother to stop talking about vomit. Having no way to speak, however, I made a motion toward my mouth as if zipping it—indicating that I needed silence desperately.

"What? You're ripping something from your mouth? What does that mean? You need me to cut the wires? Are you gonna throw up? Gonna throw up? Honey, are you gonna throw up?"

I looked at her and made a muffled noise as I covered my mouth with both hands. Taking this gesture completely the wrong way, my mother lunged at me with the wire cutters, prepared to save my life from my stomach.

Just then, a nurse entered the room, stopping dead in her tracks upon seeing my mother mounting the bed, brandishing wire cutters toward my face.

"Oh my god! What are you doing!" she cried, surely thinking that some strange woman was attacking me, which was not entirely untrue. The nurse then saw the mush that comprised my face and I saw her become as nauseated by my appearance as I was.

It then occurred to me, that in the few minutes I had been awake and fighting my queasiness, I had not yet seen my new face. I noticed a hand mirror near a sink and motioned for the nurse to bring it to me.

The nurse looked conspiratorially at my mother.

"Oh, honey, why don't you rest? You just woke up!" my mother said. I could tell she was covering something up, trying to protect me from the images the mirror would reveal.

Suddenly, I panicked. *Could my looks be worse than before?* I could feel my heart race in anticipation of seeing my new visage. I climbed out of bed, to go get the mirror myself, but was too weak and returned. I noticed that my head felt remarkably *heavy.*

"Honey, you just had major surgery. Now, the doctor said it's gonna be a while till the swelling goes down and—"

"Mmmm! Mmmm!" I shouted as I pointed to the mirror.

My mother knew she couldn't keep it from me forever. She looked at the nurse, who then gingerly brought over the pink-handled looking glass. I took it from her and, after a blinding flash of reflected sunlight, turned it around to face me.

My eyes fluttered with disbelief as I stared at the fiend before me.

Gigantic, balloonlike, like a cartoon—my face and head were swollen to massive, inhumane proportions.

I put the mirror at arm's length, trying to frame the enormity of my head within it. Little beady eyes peered out of cheeks swollen so large that my nose had ceased to exist. Dried blood caked nearly every orifice, from nostrils to mouth to ears.

But the most disturbing feature was the color of my flesh— a jaundiced yellow, swirled together with blue, black, and purple. My head was, quite literally, the size of a pumpkin. But underneath inches of puff, I could discern a definite chin that had not been there before.

My nausea returned. I dropped the mirror and it broke. Seven years of bad luck began.

While the nurse gave me intravenous codeine and anti-nausea medication, I drifted off into a posttraumatic stupor. It wasn't over. It had just begun.

The doctor told me a year would pass until all the swelling was completely gone and my new face revealed itself. It would eventually take over two years till the last vestige of puffiness abandoned me.

After several days of recuperation, Dr. Sinn decided I could be moved home. Climbing into the wheelchair, the nurse wheeled me out into the hallway towards the hospital exit.

Upon entering the hallway, it began. People stared. Jaws slacked, gaped. Mothers grabbed their children protectively as the Pumpkin-headed Beast breezed through the corridors of St. Luke's. I half expected the hospital visitors to grab torches and chase me out of town.

My first night home, the nausea was overwhelming. Trouper that she is, my mom slept next to my bed, on the floor, clutching the wire cutters in case of an emergency up-chuck that might asphyxiate her beloved son.

My mother was always an amazing nurse, which is precisely why no professional nurse has ever lived up to my expectations. Anytime I was sick, there she was, no matter the hour or her own condition.

Growing up, I rather liked being sick. Being sick meant getting attention, and attention made me feel loved. It took me thirty years and several therapists to eventually realize that pity was not the same thing as love, and that there are dynamics suitable to a mother-child relationship that are unsuitable to any other interpersonal dynamic. I tried for years to squeeze sympathy out of friends and lovers, thinking that pity meant love. Now I realize that the attention garnished from sympathy only makes people think you are weak.

Being that my mouth was wired shut, I obviously could not eat. Between my two front teeth, near the gums there was a tiny gap barely large enough to accommodate, let's say, a needle. Through this opening, this tiny portal, I would have to feed myself on a liquid diet for eight weeks. Also, any and all medications would be fed through this pinprick of a hole—mostly liquid codeine and anti-inflammatory drugs.

While I survived on a steady diet of apple juice and Gatorade, I was dreadfully weak. Because of my liquid diet I was forced to continuously drink for fear of dehydration. Every waking moment found a straw in my mouth. Being that the miniscule gap between my two front teeth was the only passageway for nourishment, I was not able to sip anything that possessed even a speck of food. No pulp, no granules of any kind would make it past the pinprick that was my lifeline.

Regardless of this fact, it became a personal mission for my devoted mother to not exclude me from family meals or occasions. I was made to sit at the dinner table, almost nightly, and watch in contempt as my father, mother, and sister gorged themselves on pot roast, chicken and dumplings, and sloppy joes. Knowing this must be a unique kind of hell for me, my mother took it upon herself to set aside my dinner portions and puree them into a frothy broth. She pulverized every conceivable food known to man.

"Dinner's ready!" she would cry from the kitchen.

Then, moments later, the roar of a Cuisinart would fill the house. Despite her efforts, it was a rare occasion that the roast beef, still warm from the oven, would be ground up enough to make it past my tiny feeding hole. Usually I would take a couple of sickening sucks, only to have the river log-jammed by a stray piece of beef or chicken pulp.

They say Einstein's theory of insanity is repeating the same mistake and expecting different results. Those eight weeks, Cuisinart could have used that slogan as a tagline for their newest ad campaign.

The insanity reached a peak when, for my nineteenth birthday, my mother pureed my birthday cake. The end result of pureed birthday cake is very much like how birthday cake begins—batter. Sipping one's birthday cake through a straw might be a nice idea, but there's a reason people bake cakes instead of drink them.

During my birthday, my extended family decided to pay me a visit to survey the damage.

My grandma, or Nee Naw as we called her, lived in a trailer park in Denton, Texas, just one hour north of our brick-and-mortar abode, with her daughter, Aunt Carol, and Carol's daughters Angela and Shandra.

When I visited my relatives' trailer park I would often observe their neighbors abusing themselves and their children. Trailer parks seem to be wastelands of any kind of information about anything to do with human relationships or child rearing. People talk about the sad life that gays lead. Well, no amount of lonely promiscuity could compare to the misery and suffering of many heterosexual couples living in rural parts of this country. Growing up in Texas, I witnessed many of the female denizens give birth to blameless children who go on to be ignored by macho, wretched husbands and themselves. If anyone has doubts about the virtues of gay parenting, I invite them to spend one afternoon in a trailer park with heterosexuals whose sole qualification for raising a child is that they got fucked.

In my parents' Ranch style house the only one that was "fucked" was me. My aunt Carol, Angela, and Shandra stood before me, gazing at the beach ball staring back at them. They struggled to contain their laughter at my condition.

"Oh, he looks like a Mr. Potato Head!" Shandra giggled.

"Do you think he's gonna ever look normal again?" Angela wondered aloud.

"He looks like he was beaten with an ugly stick!" my aunt joked. " 'It's the Great Pumpkin, Charlie Brown!' "

They all burst into laughter as if I wasn't in the room.

I learned early on in this experience that there is a portion of the human brain that believes that if one cannot *speak*, that person also cannot *hear*. It was common for most who encountered me to talk about me as if I wasn't there. I had seen this phenomenon before when my father would host one of his many garage sales. When encountered with non-English-speaking Mexicans, he would often overcompensate for their lack of English by simply talking louder.

"Do you think he's in pain?" my aunt Carol asked my mother. I reached for my notepad to write NO but, as usual, I wasn't able to write an answer quickly enough so everyone turned to my mom for an answer.

"No, it's more uncomfortable than anything. He has some nerve damage from the surgery, though. There are spots on his face that are numb and probably always will be. Plus he lost his sense of smell but they say that may come back."

My sense of smell never did come back. While I have informed all my loved ones of this, I still receive aromatherapy candles and incense sticks at every birthday or Christmas gathering.

For a while, I would make it a point of reminding the gift-giver of my odd olfactory handicap. Now, when I receive a scented candle, I simply pretend to smell the vanilla or patchouli lustily and thank the person, saying that vanilla or patchouli is my favorite scent of all time. Gift-giving and birthday parties being more for the giver than for the recipient, I don't really mind and I expect nothing less than the same insincerity when I bestow a similarly thoughtless present upon a loved one.

There are quite a few advantages to having no sense of smell whatsoever, especially if one lives in New York City, as I have for most of my adult life. The aroma of urine mingling with rotting garbage on a hot sidewalk has no power over me. Changing the cat box is a breeze. Morning breath, flatulence, and stinky feet have never been an impediment to intimacy for me, although I must diligently remind myself that my shoe does not fit on the other's nostrils. Cigar smoke, public restrooms, and rotten eggs fall on deaf nerve endings now.

Of course, like anything, the reverse is also true, for there are many smells that I've secretly mourned since my surgery. Fresh brewed coffee, Christmas trees, baking bread, and clean cut grass have been wistfully recalled. I have also never smelled the varied and sundry aromas of sex, since I lost my sense of smell before I lost my virginity. The scent of another man does not exist for me; pheromones wield no pull of attraction in the game of seduction here.

Many dangers present themselves when one has no sense of smell. I have gotten food poisoning numerous times due to spoiled groceries. The ability to smell can be quite the lifesaver, as I have been forced to realize.

For several weeks I was exhausted beyond belief. Convinced that I had chronic fatigue syndrome, those worries were dispelled when a friend walked into my New York apartment only to immediately inform me that there was a gas leak in my home. Since then, I have thought of purchasing a canary to warn me of such leaks, but instead have opted to host dinner parties to alert me to such noxious emissions. If my guests drop dead over the soup, the pilot light must be out.

While I had lost my sense of smell and my ability to speak for two months, all I could do was watch others do both. After my cousins had marveled at the Great Pumpkin, my grandma sat down next to me on the couch.

Being that we rarely had these grandma-grandson pow-wows anymore, she decided to seize this moment of muteness from me and share some rather startling observations of her grandson.

"I know you're gay," she whispered, looking around the room so as not to be heard.

My eyes blinked back at her, stunned—not just by what she had said, but that she was breaking my relatives' cycle of assuming that I was deaf as well as mute.

"Don't say anything, let me talk."

As if that were an option.

"Now, I know the Bible says it's a sin and all, but"—she looked around again to ensure total privacy—"I think all your Jesus talk is just a lot of horseshit.

"I mean, I've known lots of gays in my day. You know, I've lived a full life and I know your momma don't approve. But life ain't about sittin' in a church. It's about drinking and smoking and carrying on—living! When I was with Merle—"

My grandmother had briefly dated a very young and struggling country-western singer named Merle Haggard. Riding around in the back of his pickup truck from honky-tonk to honky-tonk, Gaylon felt a kinship with performers and sympathy for the many paradoxes of showpeople. She understood my dreams of stardom like no one else in my family. If she had married Merle, her name would have been Gay Haggard, a name which, on occasion, I have felt represents the dyslexic embodiment of myself.

"Well, Merle didn't believe in any of that crap and the Jesus freaks tried to shut him down, saying he was singing sin songs and all. Now, your momma, she grew up around all my crazy, hell-raisin' men and now she's just trying to make meanin' outta the crazy mess that my life is.

"Now, I'm not saying I don't believe in nuthin'. My momma's spirit used to visit me after she was dead. She was a full-blooded Cherokee, you know. So I believe there's something out there.

"But I bring this up cause there ain't nuthin' wrong with what you are. Hell, I've known you was a queer the first time I seen you throw a ball!"

She laughed uproariously but was silenced as hilarity evolved into a smoker's cough.

"Now, your momma and daddy tell me that you're planning on moving to New York to be an actor once all this face swellin' goes down. I think you should. Me, I've always thought I coulda been a movie star had I been so inclined. But I want you to remember just one thing when you get to New York: If anyone tells you that you can't make it in showbiz, you just tell 'em, 'Hide and watch!' Okay, now I gotta get in that kitchen and fry up the okra. Remember: 'Hide and watch!' "

Over the next eight weeks, my family took turns confessing to me the resentments each had for the other. I secretly said little prayers to the makers of the drug codeine, wherever they may be. Had it not been for that purplish drug sucked through a straw between confessionals, I doubt I would have been able to bear it.

My aunt Carol, or "Auntie" as I called her—way past an age a man might call his aunt "Auntie"—sat down and torched up one of her beloved low-tar Carltons next to her daughter Shandra and I. I took a sip of codeine.

"Well, thank God they fixed his long face," my "Auntie" snickered.

"I think his new face kinda looks like Elvis—when he was real bloated-like," Shandra observed, completely ignoring the fact that I could hear. "God, he looks really weird. His face almost looks fake—like foam rubber." Shandra spoke in a thick Texan accent, even though she grew up in California, like me, and had only been in Texas for two years.

"Dinner's ready!" my mom cried out. A moment later, the blender started.

The entire family gathered in my parents' dining room in front of a huge Texan feast of ribs, mashed potatoes, fried okra, and corn on the cob. Being that it was my birthday dinner, my parents insisted I join them at the table. I rarely got off the couch by this point, not only because I was completely addicted to painkillers but also because my swollen head weighed over a hundred pounds and was hard to support on my eighteen-year-old neck. My mother sat a large glass of pureed rib meat in front of me. I took one sip and decided instead to stick to apple juice.

"Oh, this fried okra is the most deelish thing I've ever eaten in my life!" my aunt declared. "Oh, it's too bad Craig can't have any!"

I was into my fifth week of not eating. That's thirty-five days of no food.

If we had been on a glacier in the Andes, I would have eaten my entire family and several of my own toes by this point.

"Oh! These ribs! Amazing!" Angela declared loudly.

"Have some corn! Cecil cooked it on the grill, in the husks, and it is just remarkable!" my mother boasted.

I sipped. I gnashed my teeth. Sip, sip, sip.

"Oh, Craig, it is just a shame that you cannot eat this food!" Shandra moaned as she stuffed an entire dinner roll into her mouth. She said something else after that, unintelligible due to her stuffed jowls.

That was it. I couldn't take it anymore. For reasons that I don't quite understand *bread* was the food that I missed most during those months of no food. Warm, baked bread. I had assumed I would miss chocolate, french fries, tacos—but bread turned out to be the food I longed to make sweet love to.

I got up from the dinner table, crankily.

"Now, see! Y'all have gone and made him upset!" my grandma grunted, a rib dangling from her mouth.

"Well, maybe he's just tired," Shandra said.

"Yeah, he's just worn out—his head is so big, it's hard for him to hold it up," noticed Angela.

"Well, perhaps it's for the best. This food is delicious, but he can't have any!" Auntie whispered.

I turned around to face my family. Picking up a dinner roll, I threw it across the room spontaneously. It unintentionally bounced off my grandma's nose, leaving a small butter stain.

Everyone looked at me. Finally, they saw me. I tried, in vain, to indicate to them that I could still hear. I pointed to my ears, and then pointed to their mouths, demanding that they stop speaking of me as if I wasn't in the room.

I can still hear! I indicated.

"Craig, why did you throw that bun? Oh, I know! You want me to puree some dinner rolls!"

As my mother ran to the Cuisinart with rolls in hand, I

grabbed my car keys and snuck out of the house, the sound of the blender concealing my escape. I was tired of being treated like a deaf person and I thought I certainly must have ridiculed deaf people in a past life to deserve this.

Dressed in pajamas, I drove down the road. I had not left the house alone since my surgery and had forgotten that, while my family was used to my pumpkin head and monstrous face, the rest of the world was completely unprepared.

As I drove down the road, passing cars swerved in horror as they recoiled from the gargantuan face in the opposite lane. They would catch only glimpses of my monstrous head, and I got only glimpses of their gaping, terrified looks. But those looks remain a snapshot in my mind's eye.

Too weak and inappropriately dressed to go inside a restaurant, I decided that I would go through the drive-through window at our town's one and only restaurant, Dairy Queen. There I would order a milkshake, something I knew I could drink, although what I really needed was a whiskey.

I approached the Dairy Queen, rolled down my window, and pulled up to the speaker. Suddenly I realized that I could not order since my mouth was wired shut. Not knowing what to do, I decided to throw caution to the wind and approach the pickup window.

As I pulled up, a sixteen-year-old stoner type boy with long hair greeted me. Glassy-eyed and most definitely unhappy with his job, the Dairy Queen boy shrunk back in dazed horror as my face was revealed in his window. I'm sure to him it must have seemed as if the Elephant Man had migrated to Texas and was dying for a Blizzard Sundae. It was obvious that he wondered if I was real or some unpleasant acid flashback.

Trying to communicate, I took a notepad from my car and

wrote on it: ONE LARGE CHOCOLATE MILKSHAKE. I handed it to him and he stood there for a moment as he read my order. Looking from the notes to me, he nodded his head silently. I nodded back and he went off to make my drink.

I felt vindicated. Finally I had actually communicated with someone. I had been heard. He saw me, heard me, and was not treating me as though I was a deaf mute. A few minutes later, he emerged with my milkshake. He handed me the frothy drink.

He then handed me a piece of paper. I took it from him, confused.

On Dairy Queen stationery, he had written *$1.89*.

AIDS: The Musical!

My first professional theatrical experience was in something burdened by the unfortunate title *AIDS: The Musical!*

Like most musicals based on life threatening viruses, *AIDS: The Musical!* was a charming little ditty of skits, vignettes, and musical production numbers meant to serve as both public health service and toe-tapping entertainment.

While the show took place at the "Theater Gemini," it was actually not performed in a theater at all, but a makeshift stage set in the back storage room of the Dallas AIDS Resource Center. Each week we would present our theatrical razzle-dazzle to sold-out audiences of thirty tenderhearted souls. Propped up on rickety and wobbly folding wooden chairs which had the nasty habit of snapping and breaking during the most inopportune dramatic moments, the mostly gay and lesbian patrons would sit attentively each Friday, Saturday, and Sunday night as we infused top-notch Dallas theater with a heavy dose of thought-provoking messages on tolerance and safe sex. *AIDS: The Musical!* aimed to be the kind of sociopolitical theatrical experience the NEA Four would have been proud of.

Propelled by musical numbers with self-explanatory titles such as "Safe Living in Dangerous Times" and "Rimming at the Baths," we were the epitome of cutting-edge, underground, local community theater.

Dallas is not particularly known for its major contributions to the advancement of theater arts. It is not a city like, let's say, Chicago or New York or even San Diego. But one must pay one's dues somewhere and I paid mine on the storage room "stages" of Dallas and Fort Worth, Texas.

I had no idea that there even was a theater community in Dallas when I went home after a disastrous two-year jaunt in New York City. The only theater I had experienced in Texas was a family trip to a dinner theater located in a barn in Mesquite, a suburb of Dallas, to see a comedy that was passing through town, *Love Letters*. There, my parents, my sister, and I feasted not only on the delicious chicken-fried steak afforded us, but also on the brilliant and masterful performance by the star of the show, Bill Daily, who starred in TV's *I Dream of Jeannie*.

"That Bill Daily is just as funny now as when he was on *Bewitched*!" My mother said in the car, on our way home. "We should see more theater!"

"Where?" I asked. "We live in Texas—not New York City!"

I was still smarting from my family's trip to New York City when I was twelve. That year, in 1978, my parents and I had the opportunity to see some amazing Broadway shows—*Annie*, *A Chorus Line*, and *Peter Pan*, among others. Instead, my parents insisted we see a not-very-good revival of *Oklahoma!*

"But we're from Texas! I don't want to see *Oklahoma!* I live in Oklahoma!" I cried as we entered the theater.

My introduction to the Dallas theatrical community began, oddly enough, in a Dallas gay disco called Baby's. I have always been amused by the names of gay bars, especially in smaller metropolitan areas: Throckmorton Mining Company, Pieces, Kolorz, The Male Slot, Pink Socks, Trix, BJ's, The Big Top, Bottoms Up, The Giggle Pin, Hot Pants, Skid Marx, Beer Goggles, The One Trick Pony, Midnight Mary's, Jack's off First, The Chicken Hawk, Twigs and Berries, Old Joe's, Grinders, Cherry Harvest, Piccolo's, Uptown Lady, Whiskers, Percy's, The Chopper, Bronco's, The Pacific Rim, Choices, Scandals, Attitudes, Hide and Seek Complex, Options, Persuasions, Insinuations, Tribulations, The White Swallow, Members, Fudgey's, Hunky's, Magnolia Station, The Village Station. (Why so many gay bar names have the word "station" in them has always perplexed me. As if it were a depot, a train station of gays going to and fro, arms outstretched from railroad-car windows, hankies bidding adieu to the "trix" they're leaving behind.)

While dancing at Baby's to "Venus" by Bananarama, I was in particularly good form that night. I had just gotten a great new short bowl-cut at the mall and was tossing my Dorothy Hamill hairdo on the dance floor. Sporting a blousy midriff white shirt that said CHOOSE LIFE in big WHAM!-esque letters and pajama bottoms with paint strategically flecked on them by the manufacturers, I energetically practiced some newly acquired dance steps I had studied from a Taylor Dayne music video.

After my imaginary audition for *Solid Gold*, I ran to the bar for my third Cape Cod. I went to Baby's for their famous fifty-cent Cape Cod nights on Tuesdays. While ordering my drink and deflecting passes made at me as only a twenty-one-year-old can, something suddenly caught the corner of my eye. Something very familiar.

Upon closer examination I realized that it was a pink ascot. Certainly there couldn't be more than one pink ascot in circulation in Dallas. And I was right—underneath that ascot was the first openly gay person I had ever met—Paco Butte.

Paco had not seen me in several years, not since my facial reconstruction.

"Hi!" I said as I bounced over to him.

Paco looked at me as if I was some groupie fan. He had been recently doing a one-"woman" show at a run-down gay piano bar called "Auntie Mame's" where he nightly interpreted a musical repertoire of "People," "It's Raining Men," "Feelings," and several TV theme songs.

"No autographs, please. I'm a civilian tonight."

"It's Craig. Craig Chester." I smiled. I had gotten used to these kinds of reactions being that I had had complete maxillofacial reconstruction and looked nothing like my former self.

Paco's *own* face morphed upon the realization.

"*Oh my god!* You're not ugly anymore! Oops. Sorry."

Paco's attitude towards me, like everyone's, had completely changed right along with my face. I had grown accustomed to the very people who had been rude and callous when I was deformed suddenly flirting with me and treating me like a prince.

"I have an audition tomorrow! You should come with me!" he said as he looked lustily at my crotch.

"An audition?"

"Yeah, for a musical—about AIDS," Paco said as if giving me top secret insider information.

"Wow, neat! I didn't know they had musicals about AIDS in Dallas!"

Paco and I went to IHOP for a 4 A.M. fix of chocolate-chip pancakes and the next day, extremely hung over, I returned to my hated place of employment—a time-share real-estate company called "Piney Shores."

Piney Shores was basically a bunch of run-down condos on a swamp in the humid woods of East Texas. Every week, our company would mail out letters that would proclaim to the recipient that they had been selected out of the blue for a treasure trove of riches. Having committed no crime other than to have a mailing address, a wave of joy would sweep the recipient into some internal casino fantasy as they read in big bold letters: YOU'VE WON A NEW CAR! or YOU ARE A WINNER (*insert name here*)! COME TO PINEY SHORES TO PICK UP YOUR NEW MITSUBISHI TV!" The fine print on the back, however, informed the winner that indeed they had not won a damn thing but would be placed in a "drawing" for their very un-won prizes. But no one ever, *ever* read the fine print and week after week, these optimists would load up in the pickup truck, some driving six hours each way, to the dumpy Piney Shores where their new car or TV awaited them. Once there, they would be accosted by a high-pressure salesperson trying to get them to sign a time-share contract. When asked where their cars were, or TVs, the seemingly fearless salesperson would hand them a toy car or a photo of a television set as tempers flared and marriages broke up.

My job as a telemarketer was to book appointments for this scam of an operation. People would often call, hysterical upon receiving notice of their good fortune, like a game-show contestant without the show.

"I won! I won!" they would exclaim into my headset. "I've

never won anything in my life and sweet Jesus, I've won!"

"Yes, you have Mrs. Garcia! You are a winner! When would you like to visit Piney Shores to pick up your new car?!"

Knowing that I was consciously sending Mrs. Garcia to a rendezvous with a Matchbox Hot Wheel did bother me, but I was desperate for a paycheck. Daily I manipulated people into making appointments at Piney Shores so that I could pay my rent and keep the lights on in my ramshackle apartment.

Every once in a while, I would get a call from a disgruntled "winner" who had gone to the resort, been handed a photo of a TV set, and held me personally responsible for lying to them which, as matter of fact, I had.

"I got me a sawed off shotgun! I'm gonna come and blow you away!" was a battle cry I became oh-too-familiar with during my telemarketing tenure at Piney Shores. The entire six months I worked at Piney Shores, I was truly shocked that no employee *had* been killed, both in our downtown Dallas office and especially at the actual resort. How a salesperson could hand over a toy car to someone that drove five hours to pick up the real thing and not get shot or stabbed is beyond me. Any court in the country would have found it justifiable homicide.

It was common for me to put people on hold so that I could look up information on my computer. Often, I would forgo the HOLD button for my MUTE button so that I could hear the person even though they could not hear me.

During these muted phone calls, I recognized a phenomenon that I had hitherto been unaware of that is sweeping the nation. When I would put a person on MUTE, ninety percent of the people I would be eavesdropping on would mumble, "Whatcha doin'?" in baby talk.

"Whatcha doin'?," I surmised, is what people at home say to their dog, cat, boyfriend, or baby when they believe that they have been put on hold and cannot be heard.

"I'll have to put you on hold for a moment, Ms. Durken."

"Well, you better get me a supervisor 'cause I've had it with you people! You have worked my very last nerve and I will not rest until you are all dead and six feet under!"

Then, with one click of the MUTE button, I would hear the evil Ms. Durken drop her ball-busting threats and coo to a nearby dog or baby or who-knew-what.

"Awww. Whatcha doin'?"

Even today, I find myself doing this very thing. If a telemarketer sends me into that temporary land of limbo of "Please hold," I cannot help myself. I stand there, phone pushed to ear, gazing at my cat and cooing, "Whatcha doin'? WHATCHA DOIN'! Awwww!"

I'd like to say that I quit this immoral and unethical job because my conscience had gotten the best of me, but I'm afraid no such moral convictions ever occurred.

One day, while sipping my usual three o'clock coffee, a news crew burst into the telemarketing office. Bright lights attached to cameras and a boom mike swept past the cubicles like a shark looking for a baby seal. My supervisor yelled, threatened the reporter, but the camera crew persisted, eventually winding up in front of me. A microphone was shoved into my face. I was a seal in the headlights.

"Do you coerce people into driving hours and hours by lying about phony prizes?"

Once my eyes had adjusted to the lights, I realized who was standing before me, holding the microphone. It was Rowena Krokidas—the same newswoman who, during high school, had been a belching and drunken homophobe while my high-school drama department performed at her news department's Christmas party.

At my audition for *AIDS: The Musical!* I was nervous. My scene was a dramatic recounting of a man with AIDS who is dead but doesn't know it yet. Everyone in the scene talks about him as if I'm/he's not there. The scene required me to run around waving my hands desperately in the other actors' faces. "I'm right here! I'm not—*dead!*" I would cry. "I'm *alive!*"

Also required was a demonstration of my abilities to sing and dance, which, unfortunately, are somewhat on par with that of a deaf polio victim. Still, never one to fear humiliating myself, I stood in the storage room in the back of the AIDS resource center, belting out the only song I had ever learned to sing thus far—"My Own Space."

Paco was up after me. Since there was no actual lobby because there was no actual theater, the auditioning thespians were contained in a food pantry amongst cans of beans and boxes of macaroni and cheese. The AIDS Resource Center collected these food items to give out to struggling people with AIDS. But today, it was showtime!

I entered the somewhat crowded closet that was brimming with nonperishables. Paco was doing vocal exercises.

"How did it go?" he asked

"Okay, I guess. I don't think my song went very well. But the director is really hot!"

"Well, just leave the singin' to me, honey!"

"What are you performing?"

" 'Over the Rainbow,' of course!"

Paco swept into the audition like Margo Channing, leaving me to pull up a large, super-industrial-sized box of Goya Pink Beans to perch upon. A strange, colorfully dressed woman who resembled a sixty-year-old Betty Page sat across from me, looking over her "sides." Next to her, crammed in between boxes of Fruity Pebbles, was an even older gay man.

"Hello. Are you here for peaches?" The man stretched out his hand grandly.

"Oh, no. I think the canned goods in here are for people with AIDS."

"No, I meant the role of 'Peaches,' the elderly tranny streetwalker with AIDS. I hope not, because so am I!" he said. He resembled Gloria Swanson in both temperament and looks. "Sorry, I'm in character."

Stunned, but needing to respond, I shook his hand.

"Hey there! I'm Madge! I'm up for the role of the mom whose son dies of AIDS. You know, the scene that propels the musical number about PFLAGG? Whatever the hell that is!"

I hadn't read the entire script for *AIDS: The Musical!* but I pretended as if I had.

"Ahhh!"

Madge noticed me looking at her hair. It was remarkably black. China doll black.

"What? Why are you looking at me like that?"

"I'm not looking at you. It's just so dark in here," I lied.

"That's okay, kid. I get those stares a lot. Ever since *Silk-wood* came out. I guess you saw *Silkwood*."

"Um. Yeah. I did."

"I was in it. We shot it over at Las Colinas Studios. I had a scene in the nuclear plant's lunchroom. I was eating P and J?"

Madge went on to describe what was essentially a role as

an extra in a large cafeteria scene. Later when I saw the movie again on video, with the help of the "pause" button on my VCR, there was Madge. A speck in a crowd of fifty other extras.

"Ever since *Silkwood* came out, I get those stares a lot. People think, 'Gosh, she looks so familiar!' You kinda get used to saying 'I bet ya saw *Silkwood*, huh?' Of course, they all have. I don't mind."

" *'If happy little bluebirds fly, beyond the rainbow, why oh why can't I'?"*

Through the bags of Top Ramen, we heard Paco's dramatic finish to his audition song.

"Ugh! She's ruining that song! Miss Bette Davis sings!" Peaches noticed. "I'm the chapter president of Judy's fan club and a baritone cannot sing 'Over the Rainbow'!"

A few moments later, the door to the food pantry flew open and Paco stood before us.

"A cinch! I'm sure to get the role! Okay, let's go!"

I reached out my hand to Peaches.

"Okay, well, break a leg."

"A leg? More like break a hip!" Paco muttered under his breath as he straightened his bolo tie.

"Thank you, darling! I hope we can work on this wonderful, historic musical extravaganza together!"

I looked over at Madge—who was now sheepishly eating a bag of Doritos she had been sitting on just moments before.

"I think those are for people with AIDS."

"But me hungwee!" she said, in a strange baby like squeak.

Since Paco did not have a car or a driver's license, I drove my recently rediscovered high-school chum to a restaurant called Snuffers for a much-needed post-audition snack. Once at Snuffers, we met up with a friend of Paco's—a person that would eventually become the longest, most enduring friendship of my life—Katherine Connella.

Katherine, although I did not know at first, is intersexed, a real-life hermaphrodite. Born Charles Busbice, Katherine had been raised as a boy by her born-again Christian Texan parents. When Charles hit puberty and had the unlucky occasion to grow rather large and voluptuous knockers, Charles could no longer hide that she existed between two worlds. After years of mental hospitals, hormone therapies, and suffering through the dark ages of sexual therapies, Charles eventually allowed his true self—Katherine—to emerge, thank God. As a result of this hard-knock life, Katherine is utterly, completely, and unabashedly herself. I have never known anyone in my life to care so little of what others think or anyone with such an unapologetic and unself-conscious modus operandi.

Katherine and Paco had met in a, shall we say, unconventional way. While living in the converted garage of her parents suburban home in Irving, Texas, a suburb of Dallas, Katherine made extra pocket change by doing phone sex.

When she first started doing phone sex, Katherine met and started having a quasi-affair with an actor-singer named Paul, who also did phone sex. A few months into their affair, she started working on her male voice (Randy) with Paul. He said it was good but didn't think it would fool a "real" gay guy. She bet him he was wrong. So to prove it, he dug out Paco's phone number, and, with "Randy," had a three-way phone-sex orgy.

After a while, Paco wanted to meet both of them in person for hot sex. Since "Randy" was really Katherine, she politely begged out. But Paul (being bi-curious) didn't. He was okay about it at first, until Paco disrobed.

"He was lying there begging me to touch him . . . and I just couldn't. Finally I took off my shoe and rubbed my foot against his cock. But then I freaked out. I had to leave."

After that rather pedestrian footjob, Paul broke off their phone-sex relationship. But . . . Paco had a huge crush on "Randy" and wanted his telephone number. This request bruised Paul's ego, and he not only didn't give Paco the number but blew Katherine's cover and revealed that "Randy" was, for all intents and purposes, a woman.

Feeling horrible for this twenty-one-year-old gay kid, Katherine got Paco's number from Paul, and called him that night. When he answered, she introduced herself and told him she was, in fact, also "Randy" and apologized profusely for what had happened. Surprisingly, he was very chipper about it all. "Oh, that's okay!" he said brightly. "But Paul is just an asshole. Look, I'd really like to talk with you! But right now, I'm in the middle of a three-way. Could you call me back tomorrow?"

It's probably not a particularly good idea to fall in love with an employee of a gay phone-sex line but that's exactly what Paco did with "Randy." When they eventually met in Paco's dilapidated apartment, Paco calmly informed Katherine that he was still in love with "Randy" and that—even though he knew his talks with "Randy" were at an end—he really needed to say good-bye. He then asked her to sit back down while he lay on the bed.

Against her better judgment, she agreed. Paco lay back on the bed with his eyes closed. As he talked to "Randy" he began to cry and pour out his deep feelings for "him." And then—to top it all off—he began pinching his genitalia through his pants! Katherine looked at her feet and knew where this was going. So, instead of using her feet for a foot job, she used them instead to walk out to her car, happily free of the sexual tension in that apartment. On her way home, she said goodbye to "Randy" forever, too. And hello to Paco as her friend.

Paco and I entered Snuffers and, surrounded by a cloud of Benson and Hedges cigarette smoke in the back, the formidable presence of Katherine Connella sat.

"Ah now!" Paco called out, waving to her as we approached.

"Ha! Yesssss!" Katherine returned. "I was starting to worry if you were going to show up—I know it's a long walk from the AIDS Resource Center."

"Yes, well, my friend Craig drove me!"

As I sat down across from Katherine, I had a hard time looking at her. To say she was intimidating would have been the understatement of 1987.

"So how did the audition go?" Katherine asked us as she heaved her rather large breasts onto the table.

"Well, originally, I balked at even *having* to audition! I mean I've been doing theater in Dallas for two years! When I called them to see if there were any roles I might lend my name to, the queens at the AIDS center wanted me to come in and read! I said, 'Don't you know who I am?' "

"Ha! More like *'Don't you know who I think I am!'* " Katherine laughed. Katherine was the only person in Paco's life smart and funny enough to get away with lampooning his bravura persona.

"Well, I humbled myself and concentrated on 'the work' at the audition. I'm just happy that there are truly dramatic moments in this AIDS musical. I'm tired of always playing the witty and hysterical comedies—*Funny Girl* syndrome I like to call it! I can't be bouncing off the walls all the time! But, I'm sure there will be a message on my machine with an offer when I get home—I blew them away!"

"What about you, Craig? Paco said this is your first Dallas audition," Katie asked.

"Well, yeah. But I don't think I'm gonna get it. I can't really sing or dance."

Katherine leaned into me.

"Darling, the theater is a storage room. This isn't the Lunt-Fontaine."

Peaches, Madge, and I were all cast in *AIDS: The Musical!* Paco was not and his resentment at Theater Gemini was profound. Years later, when the AIDS Resource Center burned to the ground, my first thought was that Paco had finally sought retribution for not being cast in a show that he had felt was beneath him in the first place. But he had by then relocated to Austin and wasn't even in town.

At the first rehearsal for *AIDS: The Musical!*, there was a palpable excitement in the air. Comprised of nine thespians, five men and four women, a great deal of love and commitment went into making the show as good as it could possibly be. With a production budget of around $19.95, the many musical numbers would have to succeed on the pure magnetism of the cast rather than any pyrotechnics or elaborate set pieces or costumes. But that grass-roots feel fueled the "raw" theater experience we were committed to achieving. Of the four women in the show, three were lesbians, with the aged Madge standing in as the token voice of heterosexual reason. It might be hard to believe that a sixty-year-old woman could pursue being cast in something called *AIDS: The Musical!* and yet be entirely uncomfortable with homosexuality, but Madge did just that.

"I don't see why y'all have to talk about your homosexuality all the time! Why must gays shove their lifestyle in everyone's faces?"

"Madge, you are in a show called *AIDS: The Musical!* We have songs in here about bathhouses, a simulated blow job on stage, and a musical number built around dental dams," our fabulous director, Winston, commented.

"Well, AIDS is not just a gay disease. I don't see why there's no songs about blood transfusions!"

With that we all saw right through Madge. She was involved in this production in order to advance her own Dallas acting career, not because of the message behind the show. *AIDS: The Musical!* was just another showcase for her blind ambition—just another *Silkwood* cafeteria.

I made many wonderful and enduring friendships with other cast members. Since there were numerous gay men in the cast, many of them were fucking each other, passing themselves around like a taco salad at a church picnic. That the two men in the cast I slept with both refused to wear condoms during our encounters cast a particularly disturbing hue over the production. Each night we submerged ourselves in the ravages of AIDS on stage, yet these two men looked at me like a complete spoilsport when I reached for the Trojans while their legs were in the air *off* stage. They have both died since.

I informed my parents that I had finally gotten a real acting job.

"Oh, honey, that is just wonderful! When can we come see it?!" my mom beamed.

"Well, it's kinda raw. I don't know if you'd like it."

"What's it called? We can go with Nee Naw! You know how much she loved you as that dying dog in high school!"

I gulped.

"AIDS: The Musical!"

My mother looked at me.

"Maybe we'll just watch the video."

But curiosity got the best of my parents. The night they came to the show, they sat quietly as their only son sang songs about eating ass while wearing nothing but a towel. During my big solo number, "Rimming at the Baths," their presence was unmistakable in the audience. Being that we were performing to an audience of thirty, with no real proscenium, it was as if the audience were onstage with the actors. Crammed into the tiny storage room of the AIDS Resource Center, every single spectator was fully illuminated by the "stage lights." Maintaining one's concentration while acting dramatic scenes or singing songs with a clear view of the grimaced faces of the audience was a challenge. Having two of those grimacing faces belong to one's parents while prancing around the stage in an imaginary bathhouse, singing of the dangers of rimming, is a unique kind of hell altogether. At the end of "Rimming at the Baths," the choreography required me to drop my towel briefly and expose my bare butt to the crowd as I bent forward suggestively. Linda and Cecil drove into the gay ghetto of Dallas to pay ten dollars to see me in, basically, a gay strip show set to cabaret music. God bless 'em.

At the end of *AIDS: The Musical!*, each actor had a dramatic and moving monologue about having AIDS. Mine was particularly moving—and sexually graphic in its descriptive nature. These closing monologues were the only time when we were actually directed to address the perfectly visible audience. With all my might, I avoided the faces of my parents but peripherally I surmised a certain panicked expression on both their faces. My attempts to avoid their gazes were thwarted briefly when the rickety chair supporting a rather large lesbian next to my father buckled and snapped, causing her to crash to the ground during my most pregnant dramatic moment onstage. It was not uncommon for the century-old wooden chairs we used to snap during a performance, usually near the end of the show, sending unsuspecting theater patrons to the cement floor just as they gave in to their emotional vulnerability.

After the show, I approached my parents, who stood out among the gay and lesbian patrons.

"You were wonderful!" my mother said as she hugged me, weepy. She tried to pass off her tears of worry as tears of joy, a gesture I appreciated greatly in that moment. My dad also hugged me.

"Good job! Is that man all right? The one whose chair broke?"

"Yeah, *she's* fine."

As *AIDS: The Musical!* continued, we found ourselves becoming more emotionally involved in the pathos of the show than any of us would have expected. What had started out as a somewhat implausible idea for a musical evolved into a highly emotional and meaningful experience, mostly due to the fact that many members of the audience were people in the throes of AIDS themselves. They were desperate to see images of themselves onstage and the responsibility for us to "get it right" was great and rewarding. The intimacy of the theater that at first had been so off-putting began to involve us in a more personal way with those members of the audience so in need of an emotional release. *AIDS: The Musical!* began to create a safe haven for those experiences to happen—it became a theatrical support group for all involved. And in the process I, for the first time in my life, discovered the power of theater and of acting to touch lives.

Near the end of the show's run, while performing my monologue in the dramatic finale in which we address the audience, my focus was immediately drawn to a frail-looking woman who was very obviously having the catharsis of her life. Thin, with a sprayed-in-place mousy-brown flip and a sleeveless polka-dot shirt from the sixties, her face was frozen in a silent scream of anguish. The intensity of that image, the nakedness of her torment, threw me off. I faltered briefly on-stage, while she stared at me, silently weeping. The struggle within her was great, trying to maintain any possible semblance of composure.

I continued with the monologue, about AIDS and my character's mourning his life, a life rapidly coming to an end, with great effort. I suddenly felt small, dwarfed by the reality witnessing my make-believe.

After the show, I noticed the polka-dot lady outside the theater, cradled in the arms of our director, weeping on his shoulder. As I brushed by her on my way out, she saw me and grabbed me with a ferocity I had never before experienced.

"You remind me of my son," she said in a lilting Texan accent, her face wet, her eyes focused and pained.

Not knowing what to say, I took this fifty-year-old lady into my twenty-one-year-old arms. In my embrace, the polka-dot lady cried over her son who had died a year and a half before. Being from a small town in West Texas, her husband and friends refused to discuss her gay son and his gay disease at all—ever—even in the aftermath of his death. Having not one other person to talk to about her grief, she had read about our show and driven four hours to this storage room in the back of the AIDS Resource Center to finally, for the first time since his death, grieve her son with other human beings present.

As I held her, I realized that I would always be in the arts. I realized that this is precisely what art is for, even bad art.

"I just want people to know my son existed," she cried.

And now they do.

The Crying Game

Most medical students would balk at taking a course in medicine from a failed medical practitioner, yet that is exactly what actors do. There is no way around the very disturbing fact that most acting teachers are actors who are not very good at acting. Much of their resentment at the business comes vomiting forth in acting classes and, rather than promote kooky individualism in one's style of performing, many of them are in the business to squash exactly that thing, presumably because their failure in showbiz is intricately linked to their own uniqueness, their own lack of being "commercial."

When I first moved to New York, I had come to study acting at the American Academy of Dramatic Arts. AADA had quite a good reputation. It had schooled the likes of Robert Redford, Grace Kelly, Spencer Tracy, and, later, TV actors like French Stewart and Kim Cattrall (an alumna I would go on to share an episode of *Sex and the City* with).

AADA gets alot of mileage out of their alumni roster and

I'm sure it was a fabulous school before the advent of naturalism in the art of acting. But after the advent of naturalism, every acting class in the country updated its grade curve. Nowadays, if you want to get an A in an acting class, you had better cry.

Typically, a woman is a good actress if she can cry. A man is a good actor if he can be "angry." But AADA was decidedly equal opportunity: everyone was made to cry if they wanted to excel, for crying is to acting class what the perfect cheese soufflé is to a Cordon Bleu chef. Yet I have always been of the mind that "if you cry, the audience won't" and my resistance, my protest against cheap-sentiment lowest-common-denominator psycho acting, didn't exactly make me popular with the staff.

I have always had an innate problem with authority. My problem with authority doesn't just stop at police or politicians—it extends all the way to the top. Had I been in the Garden of Eden, not only would I have eaten the forbidden fruit, I would have made myself naked before God had a chance to do so.

This innate rebelliousness does not a malleable acting student make.

At AADA, we were asked to forget everything we had ever learned about our craft and start over, a starting point that for me was the ending of my interest in their services. Rather than treat each student's natural technique individually, we were herded in and out of dance classes even though I had no interest in being a leg-kicking chorus boy; singing classes even though I had no interest in show tunes outside of a drunken piano bar; and speech classes—even though I had no interest in pronouncing the "h" in "whatever."

I just wanted to act, to express myself in an environment

that, unfortunately, downplayed individual expression. Except crying. If you cried, you were good.

There were many strategies the acting teachers would use to break down one's resistance to crying. My teacher, Suzanne, had one in particular that got her out of bed in the morning; her need to see our emotional roadkill was great.

For weeks we had been doing an exercise in class called "My Private Place." The "Private Place" exercise was an acting tool that the Marquis de Sade couldn't have designed better.

In each exercise, the student would sit in front of the class and vividly re-create in his or her imagination a most treasured, private space that represented safety and security to them. To many, it was a childhood bedroom, to some a grandmother's porch—wherever one felt most safe, most alone and unencumbered in one's life. Then, after that space had been recalled into existence, Suzanne would send the other students, one at a time, into the actor's private space to basically fuck with his head in a boundary-busting gangbang. Once the actor had been sufficiently instigated into a state of discontent, the other students would return to their seats, pop some popcorn, and sit back as the actor had a complete and utter nervous breakdown, to the delight of the class.

One by one we would enter the confines of our fellow classmates' private spaces and do things like blow in their face, pull their hair, or sing "The Star-Spangled Banner" at top volume—anything to disturb their peace.

Being that I live my life with the motto "Treat others how you would like them to treat you" I was particularly bad at invading people's space. Rather than *instigate* as I entered their childhood room, my natural inclination would be to *redecorate*.

I dreaded the moment when my number would come up and I would be forced to sit in front of my classmates and humiliate myself by blubbering how "invaded" I felt. The day my turn came I sat nervously as another student, an emotionally impervious British girl named Sharon, went ahead of me.

Sharon wore cropped brown hair, with rosy cheeks that betrayed every emotion she tried to hide beneath her proper British facade. She had the look of a girl you might see stage-managing a play in high school, like a mousy rump roast whose acne had cleared up and moved south to between her breasts. But Sharon and I were the sole acting-class rebels. She had an interest in playing the classics, and we had bonded many times in our discussions of how ridiculous and pedestrian these psychotherapeutic acting exercises were. But mostly, we talked of how dumb it was to be required to cry in order to get an A.

But as Sharon sat up front, with people moving in and out of what I can only assume was an imagined bedroom somewhere in London, Sharon's resolve began to wane.

Huffing and puffing like the space shuttle about to take off, she was exhibiting enormous resistance to giving in to what she must have known on some level to be a grand manipulation.

"Ohhhhhh," she groaned, as the moisture in her eyes grew.

I ever so slightly looked under her sundress. Was that a faint glimpse of steam?—the kind you see leaking from the rocket boosters right before the burst of fire and glory that would carry the shuttle skyward? I saw only Sharon's pudgy legs and for a moment, imagined them as two perfectly cylindrical rockets affixed to the body of the Sharon shuttle.

Her mission, and it was beginning to seem she had definitely chosen to accept it, was to release the enormous internal demons she had acquired up to this point at her advanced age of nineteen.

10, 9, 8, 7, 6—Sharon was shaking, her eyes crossed, her pits exploding with nicotine-colored sweat.

—5, 4, 3, 2, 1—*Liftoff.*

Sharon took one deep breath and it happened. She cried.

"AAAAHHHHAAAA!" she wept. Tears literally flung themselves off Sharon's eyes, squirting us, the other members of her acting class, like unwitting automobiles moving through her emotional carwash.

Our acting teacher, Suzanne, had achieved her goal and she clapped her hands enthusiastically over Sharon's histrionics.

Suzanne was in her mid-forties and dressed more like a gypsy fortune teller than a denizen of the New York theater world. Her sole credit was one line in the movie *The King of Comedy*, which, to those of us just off the bus in New York, made her utterly, fatally glamorous. She often peppered her coaching with the phrase "Well, when I worked with Scorsese . . ." even though she was essentially a day player on *The King of Comedy* and very likely never received much more direction from that legendary director than where to stand.

She immediately took charge of student Sharon's emotional breakthrough.

"Good, Sharon, let it all out!"

"EEEEEEEEAAAAA!"

"Sharon, where does this pain come from? What is your inner child reacting to?"

"My mother didn't love me! My stepfather never let me wear eye makeup!" Blub blub blub.

"Good, good, go with the feelings. Sharon, you are in a safe place. We all love you."

I found this proclamation a tad presumptuous of our Suzanne. I had only been a student at the American Academy of Dramatic Arts for three months. I didn't really know Sharon very well. I mean, she seemed *okay*. But I definitely didn't love her. Especially now that she had crossed over onto the team of the criers. Looking around, I didn't think anyone else did, either, despite their fawning looks of concern.

"Class—show Sharon your love!" Suzanne waved her arms as if casting a magical gypsy spell.

On cue, all twenty of the other students in my acting class hopped over to the ailing and weeping Sharon. There we huddled around Sharon, as she wept. She seemed to be incapable of stopping her nervous breakdown and seemed to forget altogether that we were in a class or learning institution of any kind.

"I just found out my little brother smoked pot once!" she wept. "He's just a wee thing. Sixteen!" Sharon blurted, coughing up emotional phlegm.

"You have really excelled at this abandonment exercise, Sharon. We all applaud you for letting us enter 'Your Private Place.' "

With that, the entire class clapped their hands enthusiastically as Sharon continued wailing like an Irish widow. I couldn't help but feel that we were all in over our heads in terms of our teacher's ability to conjure such intense emotional breakdowns with no degree in psychology, all in the name of make-believe. God invented nose hairs for a reason. Surely plucking them in eye-watering succession or surreptitiously cutting an onion backstage would be just as believable to those folks in the darkened house as this primordial rebirthing session. Surely this crying thing wasn't any more necessary as last week's exercise when we addressed each other as our "power animals." Mine was a tiger. *Grrrr!*

I looked at Sharon with envy. She would get an A in acting class for her Frances Farmer–like histrionics. I knew very well that my abandonment exercise was up next in class and this would be a tough act to follow, this defection. I braced myself and looked for an onion.

"Okay, well, let's call it a day. Sorry, Craig, but we'll have to invade you tomorrow." Suzanne clapped. I was next in line to ride the emotional space shuttle, and it was T-minus twenty-three hours till blastoff.

In the boys' locker room, I squeezed myself into the black Danskin tights I had grown to despise with a passion. The makers of Danskin tights should be tried for crimes against humanity.

Each day of dance class, the rationalizations would begin. My budding thespian self reassured me that dance class was actually something that would someday come in handy professionally and, if not, would help me pull focus on the dance floor of a gay disco, thereby increasing my chances of getting laid.

"Movement class" was part of the AADA curriculum that my parents had paid good money for; we did not get to pick and choose how we would like to be "molded," so an education in all aspects of performing made up the curriculum. Once in "movement class," we started with a routine we had been rehearsing for weeks.

Our dance teacher, Miss Gruele, seemed to have been employed through central casting. She was a ball-buster with a bun who claimed to be French although I secretly believed her to be German. She reminded me of certain Nazi Fräuleins I had seen in movies, only in a tutu.

"Today we do 'Solid—as a *Rock*!" She slapped an actor's ass and we all watched it jiggle like a bowl of Jell-O through his burgundy tights. "Ha! 'Solid as a Ham Hock' is what you should dance to! You are all massive bowls of blubber! Your pathetic jiggling sends me giggling!"

Miss Gruele hit PLAY on the boom box and the unmistakable beat of that mid-eighties R&B classic, Ashford and Simpson's "Solid as a Rock," began blaring throughout the dance studio—which was, unfortunately for my ego, lined with floor-to-ceiling mirrors.

As the music began, each one of us had to enter the middle of the room and do certain choreographed moves we had been rehearsing for weeks, one by one in a sort of a dance-class limbo but without the pole. I particularly hated my dance sequence, which consisted of several hip gyrations and jazz-hand moves in and out, like a bird with broken wings struggling with *Swan Lake*. The routine would be capped off by a few dramatic leg kicks, none of which would ever rise higher than my navel. I had absolutely no flexibility whatsoever.

"Chester! You are a disgrace to the male form!" Miss Gruele shouted.

She approached me while Ashford and Simpson's distinctive drum loops beat on like a tribal ritual exercise in humiliation.

"Leg kick! Higher! You look like you are kicking the ass of a midget! Higher!"

Miss Gruele stood before me and pulled my leg up as high as it could go, nearly to my chin.

"Aaaahhh! I am not a woman, Miss Gruele. My hips were not socketed for childbirth!" I moaned.

"Then show me you are a man!" As if on cue, with one leg

hiked in the air, ankle in Miss Gruele's hand, my genitals burst forth from my dance belt and into my tights.

No one had explained to me exactly how to wear a dance belt. It came with no instructions, no front and back tags. I just assumed that it was like underwear, with the larger half covering the ass. But it was on that day, in front of my entire movement class, that I realized I had been wearing my dance belt backwards for the last two months, stuffing my manhood into a thin strip of fabric intended by the manufacturers to go up my ass crack. I had assumed that I was just incredibly well hung every time I burst forth from the thin strip during a leg kick. But this time, when my manhood and balls popped out, it was with such force that I almost expected it to make a sound similar to the pop of a champagne cork.

A theatrical spotlight might as well shone on my now completely silhouetted penis and balls, which hung in my Danskin tights like an exotic doorknob. Miss Gruele stated the obvious as nearly everyone in the class repressed giggle snorts.

"Ugh! You did that on purpose, Chester!?" she yelled, dropping my leg thankfully to the floor.

"Just be glad he isn't 'Solid as a Rock'!" someone in the room snorted.

The next day I sat in acting class, petrified about "My Private Place."

Suzanne entered the room, her gypsy robes flowing behind her. All of the students sat up in rapt attention.

"Okay, class. How is everyone today? Did you write in your dream journals last night?"

Sharon smiled faintly. She still seemed traumatized by her nervous breakdown just twenty-three hours ago.

"Chester, take the stage!" Suzanne bellowed. I timidly approached the middle of the room, and faced my teacher and audience. All my life, teachers and students have called me "Chester" instead of "Craig." Perhaps because my personality suited my dorky last name better than my somewhat newer first. There are no "Grandpa Craigs."

"Well, I guess I should just—" I began.

"What is with that voice!? You sound like Linda Gray on *Dallas*! Whispery, willowy—be a man, not a wisp, Chester! There are no wisps in the theater."

Really? I wondered. *Since when?*

I lowered my voice. The only other voice I knew how to do was Tevye, from *Fiddler on the Roof*. I had played him my senior year in high school and he was my butch, albeit Russian-accented, alter ego.

I pulled up a chair and sat down. In my head, I created the private safe space—my bedroom in my parents' house in Texas. I remembered Sharon's spot-on abandonment the day before, how she had seemed like the space shuttle about to take off. I knew this was all bullshit and that all I had to do was cry and I would get an A.

As I fell deeper into my "trance," Suzanne sent other students into my private space to instigate me. They would come up, tickle me, sit on my lap, all in an effort to "invade my space." Not having particularly strong boundaries as a person, I didn't much mind.

One after the other, they intruded. I began to imitate Sharon's emotions from the day before but they didn't come. Instead, I decided that if I didn't blink, my eyes would start watering, perhaps even overflow with tears.

I am going to get an A in this class. I don't care how humiliating this is!

I sat in my chair, unblinking as my eyes burned from lack of moisture. I could feel them beginning to water. The Sharon shuttle was turning into the Chesty rocket. I would go where no man had ever gone before—exploring new horizons—seeking the unseekable. Finally, I would become the Space Man, an emotionally available astronaut.

Ten, nine, eight, seven, six, five, four, three, two—

Suddenly my liftoff was aborted by another student bursting into the room.

"Oh my god, you guys! The space shuttle blew up!"

With that, everyone, including Suzanne, ran from the room to gather around a television in the breakroom. There they stood, watching the space shuttle *Challenger* explode over and over again on television.

I walked to the window and looked out onto Madison Avenue as it lay dusted with fresh snow. While I was trying to cry for an A in an acting class in Manhattan, braver souls had exploded in the heavens over Florida. Their loved ones cried real tears on television. I looked at the taxis turning the white powder to mush. Life, it seemed, would always be more interesting and profoundly sadder than any work of fiction. I decided at that point to let life, not a school or class, be my teacher, and with one small step for mankind, I joined the others around the television set to watch the first of many televised tearful cataclysms to come.

9

Well, That Was Different

Since both of my parents were born-again Christians, they had never approved of me watching TV when I was a kid. Occasionally there were exceptions to that rule, like *Wonder Woman*, *The Lucy Show*, and *The Carol Burnett Show*—all of which, psychologically speaking, might not have been the best childhood role models if you were trying to raise an upstanding Christian father type instead of a homosexual who worships female comediennes. I especially loved *Here's Lucy* because Lucy's kids were named Kim and Craig, the same as my sister and me.

I was eleven and we were watching *The Carol Burnett Show*. Harvey Korman came down a staircase in a dress and big floppy hat, his face painted like a whore's. The audience was going wild with laughter.

What is so funny? I wondered as I studied my dad's amusement. He was laughing that high-pitched falsetto I would later adopt as my own. Damn genetics. While my dad hooted at Harvey Korman, I turned to both of my parents and, very loudly, asked: "What is 'gay'?"

The laughter stopped. My mom and dad looked at me. Even Harvey Korman looked at me.

My mom and dad exchanged knowing looks and the TV was turned off. Linda came down to the floor where I was sitting. I always had to sit five inches in front of the TV set.

"Well, Craig, gay men go into a room together, take off all their clothes, poop in their hands, throw it at each other, and eat it off each other," she said in the same sincere tone she had used just months before, when she told me my woefully neglected hamster, Happy, had died and was therefore very *un*happy.

My mother had been subjected to an "awareness seminar" just weeks before, at church. A man from Los Angeles had come to our suburb of West Corina to enlighten the house-wives about "the homosexual agenda" and the practice of "scat." "Mudslinging" seemed to be the only bit of "aware-ness" about the gay lifestyle that had stuck with Linda.

I looked at her and wrinkled my nose. *They eat poop?* I wondered. I looked to my mute father, who was uncomfort-able, but felt the need to respond.

"I met a gay guy once," my dad chimed in. "He wore lots of cologne. They do that—to hide the poop smell."

All that Polo and CK One in gay bars? Poop. In case you ever wondered.

My parents surely worried that there would come a day when I, too, might eat another man's poo.

When I was eighteen, I told my mom I was going to move to New York to pursue acting. I think she heard it this way.

"Mom, I am going to New York where I will not only eat the poop of a gay but also take penises into my rectum between hits off a crack pipe, then get murdered in a violent stabbing after which I will be surely shot and my corpse set on fire. 'Bye!" Of course, she was only half right, since I have yet to be murdered.

I moved to New York at eighteen, not knowing a soul, and lived my first rough-and-tumble New York year at the YMHA, the Young Men's Hebrew Association.

My mother was famous for her care packages. She would send entire Christmas dinners and once sent a ham, which was immediately removed from the communal kitchen by the management. It hadn't occurred to my mom that it might be inappropriate to send a ham to a Jewish-run housing facility.

While I was at the YMHA, I received a large tub of brownies from my mother. Brownies had always been my favorite Mom-made treat growing up, and this was a huge batch. I unwrapped the foil and was stamping out my cigarette in preparation of diving in, when someone knocked on my dorm-room door. It was a clown.

"You have a phone call. It's an emergency." My neighbor stood at my door. He was a Jew in professional clown school and was sporting full Bozo drag.

I went to the communal hall pay phone. It was my mother. I was terrified, thinking that the "emergency" was that someone had died.

"Hi, honey! Did you get those brownies I sent?"

"Yeah! Thanks a lot. Is everything okay?"

"Oh, yes, yes. Everything's peachy. Did you eat any?"

"Brownies?" I asked. "No, why?"

"Okay, honey, now listen to me. I want you to put the phone down and throw the brownies in the garbage." She had that sweet yet stern tone in her voice. The same tone she would use when she really meant for me to listen. "Throw

them in the garbage and come back to the phone. I'll hold."
I could hear her favorite show was on in the background—
Little House on the Prairie.

"Why?"

"Something fell in them while I was baking them."

"Huh? What fell in them?"

"Just throw them away!" she pleaded in her soft Texan lilt.

I complied. I went and threw the brownies into the trash
bin. When I came back to the phone, I heard Nellie Oleson
whining in the background on TV on her end. I also overheard my father say, "Did you catch him in time?"

"Okay, they're in the trash," I said.

"Oh, good, well, talk to you later, honey. I love you!" She
hung up.

My mother had had a tough life. Her childhood had been
full of every possible kind of abuse and she was determined
to give my sister and I a life and a family that she never really
had. But once in a while, my mother's psychological past
would creep up on her, despite her valiant efforts to keep her
demons at bay. She had always suffered "spells" and nervous
breakdowns throughout my life, but now she had religion
added into the mix. Since my mother was a born-again Christian, and was convinced my recent move to New York meant
that I would begin to rack up holy abominations by acting on
my homosexuality, she had sent a package of brownies tainted
with rat poison intended to kill me . . . and send me straight
to Heaven. This act of murder certainly would have sent my
mom straight to Hell, and in her own mind, it was the ultimate act of love, the sacrifice of her soul for mine.

She later told me that the only reason she had stopped
herself was because she remembered—moments before the

phone call—that I had told her I shared all of her care packages with my fellow dorm buddies (well, except for the ham) and it suddenly occurred to her that she might take out the entire eleventh floor of the YMHA. This is why she had told my father of her plan and he had forced her to call me. My mother sought professional help, discovered she had an honest-to-goodness chemical imbalance, and once she began taking a regimen of medications she became the most amazing mother ever. Now she actually marvels at that incident, almost unable to believe she did it. Mental illness mixed with religion can be as poisonous as those brownies were. And, at the time, everything my parents had learned about gays had been from the church.

The gay shit finally hit the fan one Christmas. While shopping in the highly affordable bedding department of a J.C. Penney's with my mother, we perused a variety of bedspreads. My mom, while scrutinizing a spun-polyester Santa Fe–style throw, asked: "Which one do you think Brian would like, honey?"

She and I both knew that Brian, at the time my lover of three years, shared a queen-size bed with me in our fabulous Tribeca loft. She had been there for a day a season before, on a stopover to Ireland—a trip she had won from an Irish blown-glass company.

"I don't know. Probably the one with the floral print."

That was it. She had me at the word "floral." We both looked at each other and started laughing.

"Let's go to the food court and get a Diet Coke!" she whispered conspiratorially. I was a bit surprised by her reaction—after all, this was the same woman who just five years earlier had tried to poison me for being gay. But the magic of modern pharmaceuticals had turned my mom from born-again murderess to a proud PFLAGG-carryin', Gay Pride marchin' fag hag.

Later, in the food court of the mall, we talked for hours as she pieced together the puzzle of my adult gay life. She asked me what she had done wrong, if I hated women, and most importantly, if she thought the enema she had given me when I was five was to blame.

Over the years, my being gay has caused a spiritual renaissance in my parents. No longer born agains, they are proud of me and my accomplishments, have tried to set me up with single gay friends of theirs in Texas, and treated my boyfriends with the respect and love reserved for any family member. My mom has even been known to frequent gay bars now, dropping my openly gay name and relishing it when one of the patrons knows who Craig Chester is.

"That's my son," she now says.

No more brownies and no more "nervous breakdowns."

I've always wondered what happened to "nervous breakdowns." They were so big in the seventies.

The first boyfriend of mine my parents accepted into the fold was named Chris. Drifting along in life in my early twenties as part of a relationship, my boyfriend had just been accepted into Sarah Lawrence College's graduate writing program and off I moved to Bronxville, New York, to become a campus wife.

While my boyfriend learned how to be a writer, I cooked, cleaned, and held afternoon teas for other campus "wives" in our immaculate and tastefully decorated apartment. But, like many housewives, I grew bored.

Being that Sarah Lawrence was primarily a women's school, there was a severe shortage of boys in the theater department to populate school productions. After finding out that campus auditions were open to the general public, I auditioned and was cast in numerous productions. One of those productions was a play written by actress Joanne Woodward, who had gone back to Sarah Lawrence late in life to finish her History degree.

Joanne Woodward was the first movie star I had ever met, but more importantly, she was the first truly gifted actor I had ever spent time with. Open, warm, fiercely intelligent, and funny, she was also remarkably normal and sane—a good introduction for me into show business, for I believe that the first celebrity one encounters in one's life sets the stage for what kind of celebrity one might become. My own insanity unfortunately throws this theory into question.

I spent time with Joanne at her fabulous apartment in New York City, an hour's train ride from Bronxville, saw how she lived, watched her every move as a twenty-three-year-old might. I saw how functional her relationships with her husband, Paul Newman, and her daughter, Clea, who was my age, were.

"You have a very naturalistic quality to your acting," Joanne said one day, while furiously knitting away. "You should try getting into films."

"I don't want to do movies. You can't be openly gay and be a movie star."

Joanne looked up from her knitting.

"Well, why not?" she wondered. "Talent will prevail—luckily we still live in a world where talent prevails."

Based on that conversation, I began pursuing film-acting auditions by sending my headshot to auditions posted in an industry newspaper called *BackStage*. Within three months, I landed the leading role in a movie called *Swoon*, a black-and-white drama about the infamous Leopold and Loeb murder of the nineteen-twenties. Leopold and Loeb had a documented homosexual relationship and that important fact had been excised from previous tellings of the famous story. *Swoon* would be directed by a brilliant first-time director, Tom Kalin, and produced by the similarly gifted Christine Vaschon, who would later go on to become the David O. Selznick of independent filmmaking.

The film proved to be a watershed and kick-started the "new queer cinema" movement, along with Todd Hayne's *Poison* and Greg Araki's *The Living End*. Suddenly I was getting two thumbs up from Siskel and Ebert, and gracing the pages of nearly every major publication from *Vogue* to *Interview* to *Us*. I could pick up magazines in the checkout lane at grocery stores and find my face there, often accompanied with an article about how controversial *Swoon* was in its un-PC retelling of something that was, in fact, fact—that Leopold and Loeb were lovers. I was caught up in something bigger than myself—*Swoon* was a part of something never seen before. For the first time, openly gay filmmakers were making films about what moved them in an honest and fresh way, and everyone was writing about it and discussing the larger issue of gay representations in cinema.

I've always believed in paying attention to signs more than having some great master plan for my career. I've followed the lead of my own life and not resisted where it took me because of some preconceived notion of who I was supposed to be. Joanne Woodward challenged me on being open about being gay and still pursuing my goals as an actor, and within one year I was being interviewed by reporters about a gay movie I had starred in.

During my first real interview, I had to quickly make the decision—would I be honest or not about who I am in relation to my career.

"Soooo, Craig. What was it like to kiss another man in the movie? Was that icky for you?" the bleached blonde reporter wondered.

For a split second, I pondered what to say. But I was so pissed off about the question, that she had suggested two men kissing might be "icky," that I realized there was no way I would ever be able to play her "icky" game and still like myself in the morning or even five minutes from now. So I used my very first interview for my very first movie to make one thing perfectly clear.

"Not really. It was probably more difficult for my boyfriend to watch than for me to actually do it. I mean my costar, Danny, is really hot, right? Now, why don't you ask me what it was like to have to murder a little boy in the movie? Or is killing a child easier for you to understand than two men kissing?"

Since I had been so open in the press, I worried about my family in Texas and what people they knew might think. Now not only were they coming to grips with the fact that their son was gay, they also had to deal with the fact that everyone else who read magazines knew it too.

Explaining this decision of mine wasn't easy. My parents had always believed in my talent and didn't understand why I would risk everything by talking about being gay.

While Christmas-shopping for my mom's annual "doll calendar" at a Waldenbooks a few years later, my father turned around and saw my face peeking out at him from a magazine rack. That month, I was on the cover of a national gay magazine called *Genre*. He cautiously perused the interview, one in which I talked about my upcoming films, *Frisk* and *I Shot Andy Warhol*, in the context of being a big fag actor. Later, at home, he confronted me with what he was convinced was "a bad business move." And a "conflict of interests."

I calmly and quickly enrolled him in a fifteen-minute crash course in Discrimination 101.

"If a person can't be the president of their company because they are gay, black, or Mexican, then that's discrimination. And the president of my company, the acting business, is Tom Cruise. If Tom Cruise were gay, he could never be openly gay, nor could any actor and still go to the top of our field."

He took in what I said, and with all sincerity noted something, that to him, was perfectly logical. "If you wanted to go to the top of your field, then you should have become a hairdresser."

Although I balked, I later found out that he was right.

Unless you come out once you're rich and famous, you haven't got a prayer of becoming rich and famous if you're openly gay from the beginning of your career, at least not yet. I applaud celebrities who come out, but coming out once you have a mansion and Range Rover isn't really the same as putting your ass on the line from the get-go. My father wanted me to get that mansion and Range Rover and in his mind, this was certainly dooming me to a life of rent-controlled apartments and beat-up cars.

While *Swoon* had been a major victory for me artistically, it qualified as an embarrassment for my relatives. I told them the film featured me in some PG-13 gay sex scenes but they didn't really hear me. All they heard was, *Movie! Movie! He's in a movie. I can brag. Sweet Jesus, I can finally brag about the boy!*

My grandmother formed a posse for an excursion down to the lone art house, seventy miles away in Dallas, to see me on the big screen in *Swoon*. My aunt Carol, cousins Shandra and Angela, my sister Kim, and my parents loaded up in our RV van and headed south on Interstate 35.

Our family van had always held precious memories—of family trips to Chattanooga where we spelunked in caves, of fishing trips to Texan lakes and . . . the Porta Potti.

My dad hated to pull over and waste time on silly things like bowel movements, so some of our most boundary-free moments occurred during a family member's use of the Porta Potti, which sat in plain view of everyone else in the van.

There was a shocking lack of privacy in my family. It was not uncommon in our home to hold a conversation with someone sitting on a toilet or standing partially nude in front of you. This disarming lack of space to yourself also applied to long trips in the RV, where at any moment I could find my mother, aunt, or grandmother teetering, in full view, on the diminutive Porta Potti just feet away, pants around their knees.

There was absolutely no shame whatsoever in this perfectly normal call of nature and anyone who begged for a little privacy, like me, was looked down upon as being uptight or prudish—a fancy-pants. Usually, things like passing gas would send the RV occupants into reams of eye-watering sniggers.

On one particularly long trip to Las Vegas, while we were all loaded to capacity in the van, my grandma Gay, Nee Naw, had pulled down her green Lycra pants to perch atop the Porta Potti, Carlton cigarette dangling in her mouth. There she sat, laughing her horsey smoker's laugh as what sounded like a sack of potatoes was emptied into the bowl of water.

"Damn! That was a bowl-bridger!" she qualified as everyone in the van burst into ear-piercing squeals.

Please, God, please let us crash. I prayed for the mothership to come and take me right then and there to my rightful, biological, big-faced alien parents.

The trip to see *Swoon* would only require an hour or so worth of driving—probably nothing more than a quick pee from my cousins Angela and Shandra. Angie and Shandra and their many children lived with my aunt Carol and Nee Naw in a double-wide trailer in Denton, Texas, that was bamboozled every spring by tornadoes. At the time, my aunt Carol worked in a home for the mentally retarded. Some of my warmest family memories center around her reenacting the funny things the retarded people had done that day.

"Just yesterday, I was walking down the hall at the mental home and I heard all this banging. I turn around and there's Tony, this big fat retarded guy, and he's standing in front of a Coke machine. Well, I'm like, what the hell is he doin'? Then I see him pick up the whole machine, like this thing musta weighed like five hundred pounds, and he is just shaking that Coke machine. Well, I run over to him and I'm like, 'Tony, what in tarnation are ya doin'?' And he tries to tip the Coke machine upside down. Now, he's a big one. Like three hundred pounds or sumthin', and I demanded that he put that Coke machine down. So he slams it down. Then, his eyes all bulgin' and crazy, he runs over, picks *me* up, and turns *me* upside down and starts swinging me. I tell him, 'Tony, I don't know what problems you are having with that Coke machine but I'm not a Coke machine and you need to put me right side up, and I mean PDQ!' They train us how to talk them down, you know, when they get all crazy-acting like that. So he sets me down as if he just isn't so upset. He points to his mouth and then points to the coin slot, you know, where you put in your money? Well, he points to his mouth and he's like, 'My toof, my toof,' and I see that he done lost one of his front teeth. Then I figure out that he took that tooth and walked right over to the Coke machine and popped it in the coin slot, trying to get a Coke or a Dr Pepper, or whatever the hell he wanted, and if he just didn't jam that whole damn Coke machine with that darn tooth! Ha! Those retarded people crack me up! It's a real important job, you see, 'cause there's a lot of *prejudice* in the world. A lot of people are afraid of retarded or differently challenged people. But you learn they ain't much different than yourself. I'd sit down with a retarded person any day over some stuffy tight-ass like Jackie O or Princess Diana."

So off they went to see Craig in a movie. Craig, who moved to New York to become an actor. He had always been "different." To my family, the worst thing you could say about something was that it was "different." The first time my grandma tried sushi: "Well, *that* was different." I introduced my cousins to pesto sauce: "That sure is different." Basically anything that was new was "different" and if it was new, it was bad.

Geared up in standard-issue flip-flops, resembling *Hee Haw* cast members, they approached the ticket booth at the UA Cine.

"Hi! We're the star's family," my grandma said.

Apparently, the balding Trekkie behind the glass didn't know that Craig Chester was a star. They begrudgingly shelled out their seven bucks each and sat down in the theater, which was occupied entirely by gay men.

In the theater they sat, horrified at the images that unfolded. Black-and-white cinematography, men kissing—*Craig* kissing men—artsy-fartsy music and editing, and no happy ending. They left the theater and drove home in silence, not knowing what to say.

My parents had told everyone they knew that their son was starring in a movie and that it was coming to Dallas. Most of them had gone opening weekend, the same as my parents.

When my mom returned to work at her telemarketing job on Monday, several of the über-Christian women she worked with shunned her. Except for one, a religious zealot whose only comment about my work in *Swoon* was, "Your son has a very lovely voice."

After I heard what an embarrassment *Swoon* had been for my family, I called my aunt to find out what she and my cousins had thought of the movie.

"Well, it sure was *different*."

Chopped Liver

One morning I woke up and my liver was on the pillow next to me, smoking a cigarette, quietly angry.

I had seen that look on my liver before—that mixture of righteous indignation and cool resolve. She was throwing me shade, and I was growing tired of her constant nagging. So instead I rationalized her anger as oversensitivity on her part. Why was she so precious? *God. Livers. Go figure.*

The abuse had been going on for months, years. We had a co-dependent relationship, something that Oprah would have loved getting her hands onto. My liver knew I had damaged her for anyone else. There would be no transplants in her future; the scars of our union would make her unsuitable for another partner ever again. The seed of her resentment towards me lay in that fact. She had given me the best years of her life. Now they were decidedly over.

"You really shouldn't be smoking in bed," I muttered, not quite knowing what to say, but uncomfortable with the silence. It occurred to me that her smoking evened the playing field—she wasn't perfect either. She had vices too, the hypocrite.

But she just lay there, dragging on her Virginia Slim deliberately, slyly.

Why couldn't he be like the other bodies out there? she wondered to herself. *Surely there's more to life than this. Alcohol, drugs, bacon-and-cheese sandwiches.*

She had seen models of perfect humans and their perfect livers in the many fashion and home-decorating magazines she subscribed to. Also, she often saw people on TV who seemed to have healthy relationships with their livers. Why had she wound up with such a self-destructive loser? It didn't seem fair.

We had tried to break up many times before, the most severe of which being a nasty case of hepatitis B, which I most certainly got from eating ass behind her back. She was a jealous mistress, my liver. I had known the threat that ass-eating held. But I ignored her needs and instead gave in to my hunger.

She stubbed out the smoke and rolled over on the pillow, gazing out at the Hell's Kitchen afternoon light. Sweetly, she recalled childhood, a simpler time when the most abuse she might encounter would be the occasional antibiotic. She longed for those days—when I had been young, and she had been clean. She had been in love with me then. But not anymore.

"Ohhhhh!" she sighed to herself, whilst intending her lament for my ears. Used to this kind of emotional manipulation, I went to the kitchen and tried to ignore her.

She sighed. Then she sighed again. And seemingly unselfconscious of how transparent she was, she rolled onto her back and sighed a third time, staring at the ceiling.

"Jesus!" I said. "Were you raised on a farm? Because you sure know how to milk things!" I yelled. Still, in my quieter moments, I knew I was being unfair. She didn't deserve this abuse. They were over, my philandering days. The jig was up.

In Alcoholics Anonymous, I learned to be kinder to my liver. I learned that I abused her because I myself was abused by another organ I didn't really understand, my heart, and was passing on that sadistic pattern. While my liver got a lot out of the year that I went to meetings, I wasn't so thrilled. I didn't much like Alcoholic Anonymous, mostly because, while the "Alcoholic" portion of the title certainly proved true amongst its denizens, the "Anonymous" part proved too difficult to maintain for some of the gossipy gays I "shared" with. Something a person might forget while qualifying in a meeting about one's hellish "bottom" of crack smoking, crack whores, and ass cracks is that most of the members of that person's "audience" will not stick with A.A. and be released into the world to spill your gossipy beans. Still, I stuck with it and eventually did meet many amazing people from every walk of life. We all have demons, but I have enormous respect for people who actually do something about them—saving oneself can be as heroic as saving another.

A.A. meetings are not for addicts, but actually for people who are not very good at being addicts. The world is populated with cokeheads, drunks, food junkies, sex fiends, love addicts, and such, but most of them do not go into recovery. Most of them grow out of it or at least keep their addictions limited to weekends. Recovery, however, is only for those poor souls who, for whatever reason, have no talent at handling themselves or their self-prescribed medications. I did not do more drugs or drink more than most of the people I knew; the difference was that I was just not very *good* at it.

At my first A.A. meeting, a homeless African-American woman bolted up from her chair to address the room. "I used to be a crack addict with AIDS and now I just have AIDS!"

Everyone clapped.

That first A.A. meeting was in a basement in a church on West Fourth Street, just around the corner from where I had my first truly disastrous night of boozing it up. I was, for all intents and purposes, returning to the scene of the crime— to the first time my liver and I had it out.

Rhonda Lippman was the only friend in my new home of Manhattan that was not associated either with acting school or with the dorm-type YMHA that I lived in. While I was not Jewish, I looked enough the part to blend in among the mostly Jewish denizens of my floor, the eleventh. My friend Rhonda, however, was most definitely Jewish, but more of an L.A. Jew rather than a New York one—her Passover meals were always composed entirely of gaseous tofu, tempeh, and bean sprouts.

Topping off at four foot ten, with large, pendulous breasts and even larger, more pendulous red hair, Rhonda was an *actress*. She talked endlessly about sexual politics and feminism and made a mean pot of coffee, so strong that I often wondered if Juan Valdez had accidentally packed up and shipped Colombia's other cash crop, cocaine, instead of coffee to Rhonda. She was an NYU student at the time and lived in the top of a bell tower overlooking Washington Square Park. For extra cash, she acted in Spanish-language McDonald's commercials. She was "The Grimace" in McDonaldland, and had the skinny on all the behind the scenes McDonaldland drama.

"One of the guys in McDonaldland has a crush on me!"

"Oooh—which one? The Hamburglar? Mayor McCheese? Don't tell me it's Ronald, you climber! Wait, does this person hit on you in or out of the Grimace outfit?"

"I'm never out of it on set. You do the math."

"So he's into fat purple blobs with fins?"

"Speaking of my last boyfriend, hardee har har. Let's go to the drugstore."

Rhonda and I hightailed it to a local pharmacy around the corner from Washington Square Park. There we ran into one of my many acting teachers, whose shopping basket was filled to the rim with boxes and boxes of contraceptive sponges. She pretended not to notice me and hurriedly moved to the checkout counter.

"Jesus, is she gonna get fucked or wash her car?" I wondered aloud.

"Let's pick up my scrip."

We moved to the pharmacist's counter where Rhonda retrieved a rather large prescription for codeine, 700 milligrams each tablet.

I looked at her incredulously.

"What? They're for my back," she said as she indicated her breasts.

As we returned to her bell tower, a wicked snowstorm began to brew in the heavens above us. Upon noticing the impending blizzard, we looked at each other. We knew what this meant. Cozy piano-bar weather.

Rhonda and I had a tradition, a penchant if you will, for the many gay piano bars that populated her Greenwich Village neighborhood, particularly Marie's Crisis, a divey, dumpy hole in the wall, and the Five Oaks, a posh, elegant speakeasy, both nestled on Grove Street.

Rhonda, who looked remarkably like a nineteen-year-old Barbra Streisand, would spend hours at the open mike of Marie's Crisis, singing "People" and "Don't Rain on My Parade!" as overweight, aging gays shouted, "Sing it, Barbra!" to her delight.

I rarely sang, although I was very much involved in voice lessons at school. Still, my shyness always got the best of me and I was happy to just sit back and watch "Rhonda Streisand" get some much-deserved validation, outside of that purple Grimace suit.

Rhonda had really been there for me lately. Deeply involved in an abusive relationship with my first boyfriend, an advanced alcoholic named Steve, Rhonda's dorm room had become my very own "battered woman's shelter."

Steve, at the slightest provocation, would often physically attack me for both real and imagined reasons. It was not uncommon for a ceramic coffee mug to be flung at my face from across the room, or to be kicked into a corner until bones broke. And I would always wind up, late into the night, in Rhonda's bell tower, with a smashed nose, broken ribs, or sprained limbs. Rhonda would dutifully take me to the emergency room to get treated and tell me that I deserved better—which goes without saying. Steve had been the man I'd lost my virginity to just months before and the singular power of that experience kept me coming back to him again and again, despite his beatings and bad breath.

But tonight, I wasn't at Rhonda's tending to wounds. Rhonda had just finished midterms at NYU and she heard the far-off echoes of the piano bars calling her to come join in their high spirits despite the raging snowstorm.

"Let's go to Marie's," Rhonda demanded.

"But it's only four o'clock. And I have to sing in class tomorrow at the Academy."

"All the more reason to practice your song with an audience!" Rhonda exclaimed.

"I ain't singing my stupid showtune in public."

Rhonda looked at me, hands on hips. "How are you ever going to be an actor if you're afraid to get up in front of people?"

Rhonda had a point. I have always loved acting but hated performing. Nothing scares me more than standing in front of an audience and not having a fourth wall between us, which is one of the reasons I am such a lousy auditioner. It's hard to imagine a fourth wall when your audience is also the person reading with you.

I took Rhonda's prescription and popped a codeine into my mouth and, after washing it down with some brandy, we went into a raging snowstorm to the gay piano bars of New York's Greenwich Village.

Happily ensconced at Marie's Crisis, I began the drinking that would lead to my very first drunk. Being that I was only nineteen and still unaccustomed to tastes appreciative of an adult palate, I turned my nose up at most alcoholic beverages and instead opted for the one drink I thought tasted good— a sloe gin fizz. A sloe gin fizz, in case you didn't know, is not sloe but in actually quite fast. It tastes very much like a strawberry Crush, or a Shirley Temple, and one drinks the highly alcoholic beverage with the same thirsty swiftness as those softer drinks, unaware of the cruel joke that lies just ahead.

Rhonda was keeping right up with me, however, tossing down her celebratory midterm martinis.

After my fourth sloe gin fizz, we decided to move from

Marie's Crisis to the more lavish Five Oaks speakeasy down the street. It became suddenly clear from my drunkenness that for the next few hours I would be "Rhonda's Crisis." Getting the distance of one snowy block from Marie's seemed insurmountable. The snowstorm had turned into a full-fledged blizzard as night fell and I boozily held on as The Grimace led me across the frozen tundra of Grove Street.

We entered the welcoming heat of the Five Oaks piano bar. The Five Oaks boasts lighting so flattering that Blanche DuBois herself couldn't have illuminated the place more beautifully with all the Chinese lanterns in China.

That night, the place was packed with other soused refugees of the snowstorm. The usual stream of Broadway singers "slumming it" graced the stage, making show-stopping love to the microphone as Marie, the piano player, pounded away on the shiny black grand piano.

Marie was somewhat of a legend in her day. A short, toad-like African-American woman in her sixties, one had the impression from her demeanor that she had seen and done it all. She always wore "Princess Leia" braids on both sides of her head, presumably to drown out the occasional bad singers that she most certainly had endured decades of abuse from. Marie seemed to know by heart every single song ever written and there was no request she could not fill—from "Macho Man" to "Man of La Mancha," Marie was a pro—a one-woman karaoke machine that resembled actor James Earl Jones in Swiss Miss braids.

Rhonda and I continued our drinking binge in the way only nineteen-year-olds can. In our corner booth, we drank more and more. The sloe gin fizzes seemed to be fizzing more quickly. I watched the many singers grace the stage.

That doesn't look so hard, I thought. *I'm a performer too. I'm attending the American Academy of Dramatic Arts. I'm . . . dramatic . . .*

I leaned over to Rhonda. Actually, I fell into her lap. With my face buried deep in her crotch, I murmured, "I'm gonna sing my song."

I pulled myself up from Rhonda's lap and delicately, gingerly, made my way past the tables that had become orange cones in the obstacle course towards the stage.

I approached Marie, barely conscious.

" 'My Own Space.' Know it?"

Marie took me in. It was obvious that I was three sheets to the wind, with a comforter thrown in for good measure. Still, she seemed used to dealing with intoxicated performers such as myself. She nodded her braided Princess Leia buns.

"Great. Love your hair, by the way. 'May the force be with you.' "

I turned to face the crowded, smoky speakeasy. I imagined myself Lena Horne on a snowy night at the Cotton Club, fifty years earlier. I grabbed a stool and sat, hobbled actually, as I prepared for my song. My music teacher at school had helped me pick out the song I was working on in class—"My Own Space," which was made famous by Liza Minelli in the Broadway show *The Act*. And tonight, I was both Liza and Judy.

The music began. I grabbed the microphone and steadied myself against the stool.

The crowd grew silent as the slow, meaningful introduction began on the piano behind me. I tried to look out past the spotlight on me, trying to connect emotionally with my audience.

"This li'l number goes out to my bestest friend in the whole wide world—Rhonda," I said, setting up the song.

Suddenly, for a moment, I saw past the glaring theatrical spotlight that blinded my vision. I looked in the direction of my friend Rhonda, searching for her table, *I'll throw her a wink*, I thought. I couldn't find her. *Where is she?*

I tried to uncross my gin-soaked eyes for a moment, looking for Rhonda.

And then I saw it. Not Rhonda. *It.*

Sitting in the back of the Five Oaks, sipping on a martini, was The Grimace. He waved at me with his purple fingerless paw.

Stunned but needing to respond to the piano music, I began my song. The Grimace had thrown me off-kilter. I had drunk so much sloe gin, and with the help of 700 milligrams of codeine, had begun to hallucinate. Beads of sweat began to form on my upper lip. The room started to spin.

" 'I don't need much . . .' " I sang, " ' . . . just my own space . . .' *Blllaaaaarrrbb!*"

Without the slightest warning, vomit projected out of my mouth, hitting the microphone in front of me with a loud *thud* that reverberated over the speakers, followed by shocked gasps from the audience and not a few explosions of laughter.

"Brrraaaaaaabbbllluuuhh!" The spotlight illuminated my second Technicolor yawn with perfect clarity for all to see. Tears poured from my eyes.

Marie stood up and began yelling something unintelligible to me that I didn't wait around to decipher. I threw my nipples to the wind and hightailed it to the ladies' room, where, hugging a toilet, I spun uncontrollably in my own skin for an hour. Terrified to come out and face the crowd, I waited in that bathroom stall until Rhonda assured me that everyone had left. I had asked for my own space in a song and had gotten it in the worst way possible.

My ten years of not being very good at being bad began with the Five Oaks disaster and ended with an eerily similar calamity on Fire Island, where many gay men have experienced their bottoms—in more ways than one.

I had gone out to Fire Island's Pines to attend an AIDS charity luau with my friends Dustin and Michael Stremel. After recoiling in horror over a roasted whole pig on a spike, we overcame our nausea to feast on its pork and pineapple fruits. It was delicious and I fought off my Filipino friend Joey in a battle over the cracklings. After meeting up with gossip columnist Michael Musto, my friend Howie Lee, and a famous photographer friend, the night was young and so were we . . . well, okay—the *night* was young.

I'm not sure who suggested it, but Stremel, Howie, and I decided that we should buy some Ecstasy. Stremel seemed to know someone who sold that particular drug at the huge disco located in the Pines called the Pavilion.

I had done Ecstasy only once before, in 1986, at Dallas's Stark Club. I had rather enjoyed the sense of euphoria the drug induced and remembered that it made me run around the Stark Club complimenting people on their eighties hair, eighties clothes, and eighties selves. I am certain that if it were not for the drug Ecstasy in the nineteen-eighties, that decade's shockingly bad taste might have ended before it began. But, thanks to Ecstasy, we were all temporarily blinded to the hideousness of lacey midriff shirts and pajama bottoms strategically "flecked" with paint.

At the the Pavilion, Stremel informed Howie and I that each hit would cost thirty dollars. I searched my pockets only to find twenty-two bucks. Needing to borrow money so that I could do drugs, I approached the one person with us that night who does not do drugs at all—Michael Musto. I've always enjoyed the company of Michael Musto and am an ardent fan of his writing. He is a great New Yorker in the truest sense and I moved to Manhattan from Texas to hang out with and be witty with people like Musto.

Still, he was a gossip columnist and here I was, an actor, borrowing money from him to buy drugs. That act, my therapist would tell me, was a form of career self-sabotage. But my therapist wasn't at the Pavilion that night. Well, actually, he probably was in there somewhere.

Musto handed over the eight dollars, although I didn't tell him what I needed it for. Stremel went off and bought our Ecstasy and he, Howie, and I gobbled up the pills like Neely O'Hara placed before a bowl of Skittles.

Michael, Howie, Musto, and I moved about the crowded Fire Island club. I've never quite understood why gay men from New York City would travel two hours to one of the most idyllic nature scenes only to spend days on end tweaking in a discotheque. Actually, I could understand it that night. Because for a brief, ecstatic moment, I joined their ranks.

About fifteen minutes after taking the Ecstasy, I noticed Musto talking to a man with a very familiar face standing near the edge of the balcony. As I approached them, I noticed he was writer Paul Rudnick. Paul Rudnick wrote the wildly successful gay play *Jeffrey* and went on to even great acclaim writing screenplays, including *In & Out* and *Addams Family Values*.

That month, Paul and I were both in the same issue of a

gay magazine, with my visage gracing the cover. We had never met before, however, until this moment.

After formal introductions were made, Paul and I both launched into the mutual admiration society that makes up most first meetings such as this. Suddenly, I felt the Ecstasy begin to kick in.

"Yeah, the magazine we were in was great. I really loved your photo. And I love your work. It's just so exciting to be a part of this whole new gay thing, isn't it? I mean, who would have thought a few years ago that something like *Jeffrey* or *Swoon* could even exist? I mean, I'm just really proud of us. I'm really proud of being gay and when I wake up in the morning, I know that I am doing something good with my life, it's a great time to be gay, isn't it? It's just such a great time to be . . . *Blllllaaaaagggrraaaaaaah!*"

I threw up on Paul Rudnick.

I turned in horror to face my friends Michael Stremel and Howie who were sitting behind me on a bench.

"Brrraaaaaaaabbbbllllubbbb!"

My friend Howie had made the unfortunate decision to wear shorts that evening and I puked all over his cute, bare little legs.

As if on cue, Stremel and Howie threw up. Apparently we had gotten hold of an extremely bad batch of Ecstasy. And unless one considers vomiting all over famous playwrights ecstatic, this drug wasn't living up to its name.

I turned and faced the horrified Paul Rudnick and Michael Musto. And then, without a word, I ran. I ran and ran and ran out of the Pavilion, the Puke Palace, down the wooden walkways, completely aborting this experience and leaving everyone else to deal with the liquefied pork and pineapple that now adorned their beach attire.

Panting, I entered a private walkway to a house. I felt the urge again and climbed off the planks onto the ground compromising the front yard of this house. Hidden in the bushes, on all fours, I vomited again and again, my body trying to rid itself of the battery acid that I had certainly ingested.

Exhausted and mortified, I crawled back to the private walkway, rolled onto my back, and collapsed in a faint. Several hours must have passed as I lay there, semiconscious when suddenly I felt something strange. It felt remarkably like a hand massaging my crotch.

I looked up and was horrified to see what appeared to be an ancient old man fondling me in the dark. It wasn't actor Hume Cronyn but looked an awful lot like him.

"Uh . . . I'm sick."

"That's okay." He squeezed.

"No, I mean I am going to throw up on you if you don't stop squeezing my balls like tiny melons."

With that, a fog machine came on and Hume disappeared into the shadows, never to be seen again.

I went back to the Pavilion and noticed that it was quite empty now. The mess had been cleaned up in my absence.

While walking along the beach to where I was staying, I couldn't believe what had happened. *Could it have been any worse?* I thought. *I'll never work again. It's gonna be in the* Village Voice *for sure. Everyone will think I'm a druggie.* (To his credit, Musto never did reveal this embarrassing story in his column.)

I realized that it was time to admit that I was no good at being bad. I wanted to get rid of the deformed dork I had been in high school and be cool, to walk on the wild side. The second I did, I realized that the dork was the guy that everyone liked in the first place. Walking along the beach, I remembered what Debbie Harry had once said: "cool" rhymes with "fool." I decided moderation was the key as waves crashed behind me.

Just then, jumping out from among some reeds, a deer startled me on the beach. The shock set off one final hurrah of nausea.

You know it's time to throw in the towel once you've thrown up on Bambi.

11

The Prince of Darkness

My sister and I had grown bored of the stuffy business dinner my parents were holding at our house.

With ten dollars in our pockets and our parents' permission to go to Arby's for dinner, my little sister Kim and I jumped into my candy-apple red Mazda RX-7. We sped off down the street, eventually going the speed limit—forty-five.

As we passed a popular shopping center, I turned on the radio. Kim and I were elated. We were just getting used to a newfound freedom from our parents thanks to my recent acquisition of a driver's license and a two-seat sportscar for my sixteenth birthday.

Diana Ross's "I'm Coming Out" began blaring over the car speakers.

"Oh my gosh! I love this song!" I screamed, reaching for the dial and turning it up full blast. It was 1981 after all, and I had a particular love for this song for reasons that didn't make themselves quite clear until much, much later.

"Me too!" Kim yelled over the disco beat. She also loved

this song for reasons that didn't make themselves quite clear until much, much later.

Suddenly, in front of Kmart, a large tank of a car bounced over the median in the road and into oncoming traffic. With only a split second's warning, I slammed on the brakes but it was too late. The tiny two-seat car my sister and I sat in literally exploded around us. Metal, glass, and debris swirled around us in a whirlwind as we were suddenly packed into a human sardine can.

My legs pressed up against me, I was dazed. My forehead had hit the windshield, evidenced by a little starlike pattern in the glass. Looking over at my sister in the seat next to me, however, I could barely believe what I saw. There she was, a seven-year-old girl with a face replaced by torrents of deep red blood. She sat upright, motionless, in the passenger seat.

"Kim! Kim!" I squeaked.

But my sister sat there as the contents of her veins emptied themselves in a cascade down her face. I could discern no eyes, the color of her face uniformly red from top to bottom. A large hole faced opposite her in the windshield and I realized she had gone through the windshield and then returned to her seat, her face pulp. It looked as though a cannon ball had been shot from inside the car through the windshield; it was perfectly round, the shattered imprint of a child.

I got out of the car, hysterical, screaming for help. Many people had witnessed the accident and were standing on the sidewalks staring, not knowing whether to involve themselves in our dilemma. I looked at the car. It was barely there. What used to be the hood of the car was now gone, condensed like an accordion into the dashboard. The headlights were inches away from the front windshield.

Even though the car was a mangled slab of metal and wires,

somehow the power supply to the radio remained uninterrupted. While this nightmarish scenario unfolded, "I'm Coming Out" by Diana Ross still blared in the background, echoing off the fast-food restaurants and beauty salons in the strip mall that served as an amphitheater for this unfolding tragedy.

My sister lay bleeding. I stood and looked at the people staring, who refused to help. I pounded my fists on the roof of the car. "Help me! Please! My sister is in the car!" I cried.

A man from our church, who had been on a pay phone, ran to my aid. Helping me pry my lifeless sister from the wreckage, we moved her to the street curb. Blood ran down her face, down her chubby little legs, and dripped off her toes, forming a tiny stream in the gutter. She was wearing flip-flops on dirt- and blood-caked feet.

I held Kim's hand as we huddled together on the curb outside the strip mall. I was convinced I'd killed her, or worse, blinded her for life. I begged for her forgiveness. She didn't speak, but then slowly squeezed my hand responsively, a gesture that seemed mature beyond her years. A twelve-year-old boy stood across the street, taking pictures of me screaming, crying, and of my sister almost bleeding to death on a curb in front of a 7-Eleven.

Almost immediately, the police showed up and the Diana Ross song began to dim, muted by the sounds of sirens. Rushed to the hospital, my sister's nose was reattached. A silver dollar–size piece of glass was removed from her forehead. Her face resembled a patchwork quilt for weeks until the stitches were removed.

———

Since that defining experience, Diana Ross would, through no fault of her own, symbolize a car crash to me. It was only fitting, considering the irony that has pervaded my existence, that I would work with the woman who unwittingly serenaded the worst experience of my early life only twelve years later.

I received the screenplay for *Out of Darkness* while staying in Los Angeles, in between working on two independent films—the wistful comedy *Grief* and the fist-full drama *Frisk*.

When my agent called about *Out of Darkness*, I was happy to go in on it, for no other reason than breaking the strange cycle of five-letter, one-word movie titles collecting on my résumé. The role in the TV movie was small, but the producer was superstar Diana Ross, who would also star in the film—her first role since 1978's *The Wiz*. The anticipation of this megastar's return to thespianism ran high.

I got the script and prepared for my meeting.

When I walked into the audition for *Out of Darkness*, there she was—Diana Ross—in the flesh. My agents had not told me that the superstar would be at my audition and, after recoiling in horror, I shook her hand and sat down in front of her.

"Hi. I'll be reading with you today." Diana Ross smiled.

I smiled that *Great, I act with superstars every day* kind of smile, but wanted to kill my agent for not warning me she would be there.

Her back was to a large table of what I assumed to be ABC executives and the like. I sat down in a small folding chair opposite the diva and had never felt more like an indie-film actor in my life.

Centering on an end-of-her-rope schizophrenic, Paulie Cooper (Diana Ross), the TV movie focused on one woman's journey out of madness and into sanity thanks to treatment and a new wonder drug called Cloazapine. Auditioning for the role of Bill, I would make up one-fifth of Paulie's circle of similarly schizoid pals in the mental hospital where she seeks treatment. In the scene I was auditioning with, my character Bill relates to Paulie how he became "sick." It was a good monologue, quite sad and disturbing and sweet.

After I got the part, I called my folks to tell them the news.

"You tell her I want my money back!" my dad said on the phone.

"What?"

"Diana Ross! I went to see the Supremes in '67 and she never even showed up to her own concert! Tell her I want my money back! Thirty-two dollars!"

My mom got on the phone.

"Congratulations, honey! So what was she like? Is that her real hair, 'cause me and your Nee Naw have a bet going. I think it's a permanent weave but she thinks it's wigs and that she's totally bald."

My parents were relieved that I was finally appearing in something mainstream. They had never really looked at any of my independent films as legitimate reasons to rejoice.

A few months before I got the part, I had traveled to Dallas to attend the premiere of my movie *Grief* and I brought my parents to the glamorous albeit indie premiere to see me, their son, star in a feature film.

As I walked into the theater, I was asked for autographs, told how brilliant I was, and applauded during a Q&A session after the film with a sold-out audience. It was the kind of adulation and approval most parents pray for.

But on the drive home, neither of them mentioned the

movie or my performance in it at all, much to my chagrin. *Grief* was an art film to them and no amount of star treatment of me would make them think differently. When we arrived home, my father flipped on the TV and we sat down.

"Oh my gosh! It's Lisa!" my mom screamed, gesticulating wildly to the screen.

My actress friend Lisa LoCicero flashed onscreen for a millisecond in an American Express commercial. Lisa had no lines in the commercial. Her performance consisted of nothing more than a coquettish smile. But she was on TV and to my parents, TV is success.

"Now, why can't you do something like that?" my mom suggested enthusiastically.

"A TV commercial?"

"Yeah! I bet Lisa made a lot of money off of that spot!" my dad agreed.

To my folks, who only care that I am cared for, housed, and fed, money is success. Not reviews or magazine interviews or traveling to film festivals around the globe for free.

Success to a parent also includes lots of bragging.

The unusual situation I've found myself in is that, normally, starring in a movie is to most people the penultimate status symbol, even a small movie. To have a son who is an actor beat the odds and get leads in movies would for any parent be the source of unbridled pride. When that film came to town, the parent would likely tell everyone they know, even people they don't know, informing them of where it was playing, perhaps even handing out xeroxes of show time information. That is the normal reaction in a country that revolves around movies and celebrities. But *Swoon* and *Grief* were most definitely gay movies at a time when no such thing existed so, instead of bragging about my movies playing in Dallas, my parents, at the time, worried that someone might find out I was in them.

But now all that was about to change. Now their son had not only gotten something "legit" but something on TV and with someone they could brag about me working with. They told everyone they knew that I was "starring" with Diana Ross, even though my role amounted to not much more than a bit part.

When my friends found out I would be working on a TV movie with Diana Ross, they were less enthusiastic. It seemed every gossipy fag in town had heard a story about the star.

"I heard she threw a tantrum when someone called her Diana instead of 'Miss Ross'!"

"I read she pulled Mary Wilson's hair!"

"She might throw a tantrum and pull your hair!"

"She might throw a tantrum and pull her own hair!"

The stories went on and on and while I wrote them off as stupid innuendo, I didn't know what to expect on the set. The way my queeny friends described her, I half expected to show up on set only to find her with an open hand held precariously over her head at all times like a claw, ready to pull.

Regardless of my nerves, I began to do research for my role in *Out of Darkness*.

One of the joys of being an actor and a writer is that I get to experience realms and worlds I might otherwise never encounter. Researching a role or a screenplay is my favorite part of the job and I treated this TV movie like any other role I had fleshed out. Sure, the part was small, but I had a couple of good scenes and an entire scene devoted to a monologue my character has on a train with Diana.

My agent called me with the dates I would be working,

which would amount to roughly two weeks on the set. There would be no rehearsal, something that truly concerned me, considering the responsibilities of portraying a mental illness. All the movies I had done had scheduled some rehearsal time before we shot. In place of rehearsal, I received a seventh-generation video from the producers—a documentary about schizophrenia. This documentary was all the preparation thought necessary by the producers of the film. Not satisfied with this futile attempt at research, I decided to take matters into my own hands. My boyfriend at the time knew a psychiatrist in Brentwood named Frank. I called him and we met several times to discuss schizophrenia. I found out a great deal about this disease.

Schizophrenia is a serious medical condition, I learned. Affecting nearly one in every one hundred people, this mental illness is particularly insidious, for it usually preys on highly intellectual folks just as they realize their potential. It usually strikes around the age of nineteen, although it can rear its schizoid head at any time. The most common misperception of schizophrenia is that the afflicted vacillate between highly different personas—Suzy the homemaker one minute, Vanessa the street 'ho the next. I have no idea when multiple personality disorder became a pseudonym for schizophrenia but I have a feeling Sally Field had something to do with it.

The interesting thing about playing a schizophrenic would be that, to the naked eye, one might not spot a schizophrenic in a roomful of people. They blend in quite nicely on the outside for it's *what* they say, not necessarily *how* they say it that makes them identifiable as nuts. This would be especially challenging as an actor for the symptoms of the disease are very subtle. But subtle I like. When I first got the role I was worried that I'd be swinging from the chandeliers of the mental home like a banshee or being hung upside down while being told to hold my water by Diana Ross.

Frank was enormously helpful. After many visits to his lovely home, I became friends with him and his pet pig, Kiki, three hundred pounds of monstrous hairy flesh that lived in the bushes in his backyard. Kiki the pig looked something like a creature from a *Star Wars* movie. So fat and beastly was she, her brow hung down over her eyes, making her blind as a bat.

While I petted the snorting, blinded porker, Frank told me what side effects the drug my character, Bill, would experience on Cloazapine. Now I knew about the illness and felt much more confident to go before the cameras.

The day before I was to appear on set, I got a call from my agent. A very specific call.

"When you show up tomorrow, you've been instructed by the producers to refer to Diana Ross only as 'Miss Ross.' "

Gulp. I touched my hair unconsciously.

When I arrived on set, a mental hospital in Camarillo, California, I saw a face that looked wonderfully familiar. It was actress Lindsay Crouse. I immediately introduced myself.

"I am such a big fan. I saw *Daniel* eight times in high school." *Daniel* is a movie about the Rosenbergs who were executed for treason in the fifties, was directed by Sidney Lumet, and is possibly the most morbidly depressing cinematic experience this side of *Shoah*.

"You saw it eight times in high school? Jeez. Were you a depressed teenager?"

"Oh, yes."

As we drove to the set together, I found out that Ms. Crouse would be playing the role of the therapist who helps Miss Ross and the rest of us out of darkness.

I was relieved. Seeing an amazingly talented actress such as Lindsay Crouse on set made me think this project was going to be top-notch. She reeked of integrity and had even been married to writer David Mamet, whose work I also enjoyed at times. I relaxed.

As I entered the compound that comprised the mental home, I was greeted by an assistant director, who pointed me in the direction of the wardrobe trailer where I would be costumed as my character Bill.

In wardrobe, I was dressed in corduroys and many, many layers. The costume woman then draped me in a ratty cardigan sweater. I burst into a sweat, being that it was summertime.

"Is it supposed to be winter in this movie?" I asked, confused.

"No. You're mentally ill," she remarked, not looking at me.

"So, because I'm mentally ill, I'm cold all the time?"

"We got most of the schizophrenics in cardigans."

My first warning bell went off as she went to find another actor—her desire to warm schizophrenic bodies great.

I meandered towards my trailer, which was really just one big trailer sectioned off into five separate little cubicles resembling rooms in some mobilized gay bathhouse.

As I approached the steps leading up to my diminutive vestibule, I noticed a rather attractive young woman sitting on the steps next to mine. She had a dazed look on her face, not unlike mine.

I approached her. By the way she was smoking, I realized she was as nervous as I was.

"Hi, I'm Maura. I'm playing Meg."

"I'm Craig. Playing Bill."

We looked at each other for a beat.

"Do you know what you're doing?" she asked me.

"No. There was no rehearsal," I said, my face dropping. "Did you watch the tape they sent us?"

"Yeah." She eyed my layers and my cardigan. "Aren't you hot in all that?"

"Yes. I'm wearing a sweater because I'm mentally ill and fragile. I didn't know this but mentally ill people are always cold."

Maura and I talked about schizophrenia. She had done some research on her own but the concern I had was this: many of us were portraying the same illness. With no rehearsal and no discussion beforehand, would we, the supporting characters, be interpreting schizophrenic behavior truthfully and the same? Like a limp, all of us should be limping the same way, right?

Before we knew it, Maura and I were whisked to set to shoot our first scene, a scene which, unfortunately, centered around me.

For reasons I still do not understand, the Camarillo state mental hospital has a functioning bowling alley on its premises. In this scene, Miss Ross, Maura, our schizophrenic chums, and myself go bowling. Miss Ross is about to roll her ball down the lane. My character, Bill, thinks that she will score a strike using the "telepathy" of his similarly crazy friend Mike.

The scene consisted of only one line and it was mine: "Mike, telepath a strike!"

Miss Ross stood up front and gave us a friendly wave hello as Maura and I entered the bowling alley. She seemed so sweet, I immediately thought my gossipy friends were full of shit—I looked at her nails and saw no traces of human hair.

It had been decided that all the extras in the scenes at the hospital would be *actual denizens* of the mental hospital.

While the crew of the movie was mostly white men, there were a few African-American women that populated the crew. Nearly every one of them was asked for their autograph by the mentally ill extras, for each time a black female crew member walked by, I would hear the inmates whisper, "There she is! Diana Ross!"

Maura and I sat down in the pit, where our characters would be keeping score of the bowling game. Once in our places, the director, who never even introduced himself to me, yelled "Action!"

Before I knew it, I was in the scene as the camera moved on a dolly towards me.

"Mike, telepath a strike!" I whispered to the actor playing Mike.

"Cut!"

The director approached me for the first time. He was an older man, in his seventies and wore a beret and smoked a cigar.

"Yeah, Bob—"

"Um, my character's name is Bill."

"Yeah, right. Okay, look Bob, if you could wait just a little longer before saying your line."

"Oh okay, sure."

He began to walk away, then returned.

"Also, do you think you could be more—*odd?*"

"Okay," I said, having no idea what he meant yet too in-timidated by the situation to rock the boat for silly things like explanations. Several of the extras, mental patients, milled about like zombies. His comment bothered me because many of them were within sufficient distance to hear the "odd" statement.

"Sound. Speed. Action!"

I felt the camera on me, moving closer in my peripheral vision. I was looking at Miss Ross's bottom as she stood, off camera, prepared to bowl.

"Mike, telepath a strike!" I said the line almost exactly as before, my "oddness" interpreted as a kind of nervousness, knowing nothing of what "odd" might mean to this stranger directing me.

"Cut!"

I sighed. I knew that all I had given him was a jittery re-telling of my previous take. He approached me.

"Bob, look. Can you maybe—slur your words?"

"Slur my words?"

"Yeah. You know, like you're mush-mouthed?"

"Um, sure."

"Back to one!" the AD yelled.

Something was not right. I had researched schizophrenia and never heard of slurred speech as a symptom. Still, this was my first mainstream experience as an actor. I wasn't going to rock the boat.

"Action!"

The camera moved towards me.

"Mmmarrrkk, tellllepppaaaattthh aaa striiiiiiiike!"

"Cut!"

"Back to one!"

The director approached me, frustrated.

"Could you do it so that we can still understand the line?"

The director was starting to get annoyed with me—as was the crew. I realized in that moment exactly where I fit on the totem pole and it wasn't at the top. Granted, I had only a few scenes in the movie and it wasn't about me. I knew that. But judging from the loud and pointed sighs from the crew, I realized that actors in mainstream movies with tiny parts should never waste more than two takes to get it right. This was my third.

"Can we get some drool for Bob?" the director asked a makeup woman.

"Fly in the drool!" the AD shouted.

I looked at a particularly sweet schizophrenic who was moonlighting as an extra. She had heard this comment, in fact everyone had, and I was suddenly very embarrassed for us, the sane folks. I realized that these directorial notes were not truthful to schizophrenia and that I was being directed to play a mentally retarded person in a lowest common denominator way. I thought of yokels in the Midwest watching the TV movie and laughing at us, the "retards." Knowing for a fact that I was not hired to play a retard but a schizophrenic, I decided to speak my mind.

As the makeup woman was applying drool to the corners of my mouth, I stopped her. "Um, excuse me."

The director turned towards me, almost surprised to hear me speak.

"I don't think my character would be drooling or slurring his words. You see . . ."

"Huh?"

"Well, schizophrenics don't slur their words like someone with, say, Down's syndrome. I understand how the Cloazapine I'm taking might make me drool, but I'm just worried that it might come off as a tad sensationalist or exploitative to have me drool and behave like a person who is retarded."

The director stared at me. The makeup woman hovered

over me, her "drool" dangling precariously on the end of a Q-tip, waiting for a lip.

With that, the director simply rolled his shoulders and walked away. From that moment on he never spoke to me, or gave me another direction.

In the middle of shooting *Out of Darkness*, somewhere out in Neverland, Michael Jackson was served with a lawsuit for allegedly diddling a little boy. The result of that accusation had far-reaching consequences—all the way to our little TV movie set. There, the cast and crew had the unfortunate experience of being accosted daily by roving paparazzi and reporters due to the legendary surrogate-momma status of Miss Ross with Mr. Jackson, because he was "Nasty."

Reporters would be held at bay by police barricades as they screamed at our star.

"Diana! Any comment on Michael Jackson's lawsuit?"

"Miss Ross! Has he confessed to child molestation to you?"

"Diana! Was Michael Jackson molested as a child?"

"Did you ever pull Michael Jackson's hair?"

I have never understood the strange process of reporters screaming out questions to an unwilling interviewee. Has any celebrity or influential person ever, in the course of human history, ever actually responded to such hurled and abusive questions? Probably not, yet the pursuit continues pointlessly.

This prurient interest and manic "need to know" did not belong only to the paparazzi. My mother was just as deeply concerned.

"Did you talk to Diana Ross about Michael Jackson? What did she tell you?" Linda inquired over the phone.

"Oh, well, actually, Mom, she and I have breakfast each morning, holding hands and giggling over how close we've become. We're so busy sharing little inside jokes and intimacies that I guess I forgot to ask over our morning grape-fruit, 'So, hey, hon, did your friend Michael Jackson blow that ten-year-old boy? You can tell me—I am, after all, Bill, a glorified extra!' "

"Now, you don't need to be smart. Well, can you at least find out if her hair is real?" my mom laughed.

"Mom, she walked into her split-level nuclear-powered trailer with long hair and walked out with short. Does that satisfy you?!"

"Ooooh!" I heard her yell out to my grandma. "It's both! Wigs *and* weaves!"

In the background I heard my father yelling across the room to the phone my mother held: "Tell her I still want my money back!"

Frustrated by how things were progressing with the movie shoot, I called Fred, the psychiatrist. I thought if for no other reason, he could give me some free therapy on how to deal with the stress of being directed as a retard.

When he answered the phone he sounded very distraught.

"Kiki was walking around last night, slipped, and drowned in my pool," he whispered sadly. "There's a crane here pulling her out right now."

After my effusive condolences and somewhat futile attempts at speculation on Kiki's iffy afterlife, I hung up and went back to the set. As I walked back to my bathhouse trailer I couldn't help but imagine what Kiki, the pig so fat she could not see, had experienced in her final few moments here on Earth. Had there been a struggle? Did she try desperately to move her stumpy, unmovable legs in a last burst of aerobic, lifesaving energy? I was sad for both Fred and Kiki. And for myself. I was drowning, too, and a only a slender 145 pounds.

The following day was my big scene. The scene in which everything revolved around me and my character, Bill.

It just so happened that my big monologue would involve the most technically complicated shot of the entire TV movie.

In the scene, Diana Ross, Lindsay Crouse, Maura, and I would be traveling to the aforementioned bowling alley on our "field trip." The scene would be shot while we were loaded onto a commuter train at L.A.'s Union Station and would involve a hundred extras packed into our railroad car.

Before every take of my monologue, the entire train would have to start moving, so as to film the motion outside the windows. At the end of every take, the train would stop. Then when the director called "action" again, the train would go backwards to get the motion outside. The entire day we went back and forth over the same quarter mile of railroad track downtown.

The pressure of having an entire train and hundreds of people hanging on your every word, every syllable is something they do not teach you in acting school. And anyone who's ever worked with me knows that I am my best on my third take.

The first take, the train began rolling, I began my monologue and choked on one of my lines. I often flub my lines on the first and second takes, especially with no rehearsal.

"Ahhh! CUT! Back to one, for chrissakes!" the AD yelled into a walkie-talkie.

An entire train had to slow down and stop. Then, once it had, we reversed direction and began rolling again. Beads of sweat formed on my entire body, yet no makeup woman was swooping down to powder my face or touch up my makeup. Miss Ross, who had no lines in this scene, was being powdered, lined, glossed, and buffed next to me as my face began to resemble Tammy Faye Baker at a screening of *Old Yeller*. I was Bill, a nobody, and while this scene was about my character, it was definitely not about me. All that was expected of me was to get my lines out in comprehensible English, nothing more.

I flubbed a line again. Everyone, the extras, the cameraman, groaned.

"Back to one! *Goddammit!*" the AD yelled.

The entire train slowly ground to a halt.

I was about to cry. I have never felt so unpopular. Ever. And there's lots of competition for that title. I knew, however, that I was a third-take wonder, and the next one would be "it."

While the camera reloaded, I chatted with Miss Ross, who was sitting next to me on the train. She was a very nice and sweet lady, very approachable and highly professional, much more so than some of the extras surrounding us.

This was the most in-depth conversation Miss Ross and I had. She talked about missing her husband and family back East. She mentioned she was staying in Venice Beach during the shoot. Then she started talking about producing this movie.

"I really don't want to exploit these people. That's why I'm producing it. Schizophrenia is a serious illness."

I was glad we were talking about "the work." It was the first time I had heard anyone talk about what we were doing in the two weeks I'd been on set.

"Oh, I know! It affects one in a hundred people. If you

think that each of them has a dozen family members, that's a lot of people affected by this disease. And they are going to be watching," I said.

"Yes, exactly. That's why, more than anything, I just don't want this TV movie to be exploitative."

The train began rolling again. I geared up for my dramatic monologue, but this time I felt confident. It was my third take and talking to Miss Ross really had given me a boost, centered me in the importance of what we were doing. She didn't want to exploit schizophrenia and really cared about portraying the illness with integrity and sensitivity. So did I.

I began.

"Yeah, when I was nineteen, my life began to fall apart. Suddenly, I wasn't me anymore. I was me, but wasn't. Then, as time went on, the voices began—at first I thought it was God talking to me, or Jesus, and that I had been chosen to hear His messages. I waited for Jesus to come and take me home, so, I drove out to the desert to see my Uncle Hahn. I knew it was irrational, I know, I know, call me crazy, but the voices started to tell me to do things that—"

"*Aaaaahhhhhh! Aaaeeeeeeiiiiiiiiiiaaaaahhh!*"

Loud screaming interrupted my monologue, which was going perfectly. I jerked my focus to Diana Ross, who was crouching on her seat, batting imaginary flies buzzing around her head. She pulled on her hair and screamed some more.

"*Aaaaaaaaaayayayayayyayahhh!*"

Silenced by the screaming, and realizing the cameras were still rolling, I had no choice but to stop my monologue and go with this unplanned and unexpected improvisation of hers. Visions of *Lady Sings the Blues* danced in my head.

Diana Ross continued with her focus pulling histrionics until the camera ran out of film. Everyone applauded her certain-to-be-nominated-for-an-Emmy improvisation. The director came over and hugged her.

"Good work, Diana. Woo! That was intense!"

Assuming that we would be going back to one, so that I could actually do the monologue that this scene was written for, that I was hired for, the director instead yelled "Okay, moving on!"

Shocked and dismayed, I barely knew what to do. This scene had been my character's only real scene and, thanks to an upstaging legend, it was not going to happen.

The woman whose voice had symbolized a car wreck to me as a teenager now represented a train wreck. She took away my only scene in a movie I prepared and worked on for weeks. But I'll give her one thing. She never pulled my hair.

12

You'll Never Eat Ass in This Town Again

While I was having dinner at Martin Scorsese's New York townhouse one night, he asked me why I was living in Los Angeles.

It was Christmas Eve, and I was visiting New York while living at the time in L.A. I had gone to the airport, intending to go to Texas for the holiday, only to be denied admission onto the plane. Some screwup at the airport regarding my ticket.

Taking pity on the fact that I would definitely not be "home for Christmas," my friend Illeana Douglas and her then boyfriend Marty invited me to his place at the last minute so I wouldn't be alone. The subject of my living in L.A. at the time came up over dinner.

"Well," I said, "I feel like I have to figure out how the business works for me as an actor. I need to learn how to play the game." I had made only two movies at this point, *Swoon* and *Grief*, the latter of which I had worked with Illeana on.

He looked at me.

"That's bullshit. You shouldn't be thinking of this as a business—you're an actor—an artist. Let your agents think about all that stuff."

"But, I just feel that—"

"Look, artists have personal demons. I became a director because through my work, I could learn how to control the demons, turn them into something positive, you see? If you start to think of what you do as a 'business' then the demons will control *you*."

Easy for you to say, Mr. Million-Dollar Brownstone, I thought. Still, he was right. I have been lucky in my life and career to have the benefit of advice from great artists such as Scorsese. While I don't necessarily believe in role models, I do believe in the beneficial wisdom of those who have done what you wish to do for yourself. My efforts to take advice such as this have sometimes succeeded, often times failed due to things like fear, poverty, and the constant chatter of people more scared than I. Still, the balance between artistry and showbiz has been a confusing one for me, but I have learned two things in my life: there is a difference between sex and making love, and there can be a difference between acting and working as an actor.

Like many actors, I have disdain for the wholly non-creative task of auditioning. When an actor friend of mine tells me they actually love to audition, I'm always shocked and somewhat skeptical. It's probably no accident that these are also my actor friends who regularly book jobs. I have tried every possible mental form of gymnastics to "trick" myself into liking auditions, but I've never been very good at pulling one over on myself.

You might wonder why so many horribly bad actors wind

up gracing the screens of your TV and multiplex. This is because many bad actors are good auditioners and many great actors bad auditioners. To most actors who possess a reverence for acting as an art form, and a collaborative one at that, walking into a fluorescent-lit office and dropping off a bon mot of brilliance is rather like asking Picasso to come by for a five-minute doodle. If doodles are the extent of your talent, then you are almost guaranteed to book jobs because most folks like doodling.

I have, in my life, been a terrible auditioner. My main problem has not been that I am not a talented actor or that I have not been right for roles. My greatest handicap has been that I am unable and unwilling to think of what I do as a commodity, though not for lack of trying. My attempts at crossing over into more mainstream fare have often failed miserably.

In the studio system, there were no auditions. People screen-tested on a set, not in a cramped cubicle, and the unforgiving medium that is videotape was not involved. You were lit, filmed beautifully, had hair and makeup people slave over you, and you got to act with other actors.

Most casting atmospheres are sensitive to the needs of the actor. But once in a while, I will go into an audition, emotionally prepared to play a dramatic scene, only to have the chipper casting people chat me up endlessly about the most inane and distracting topics of conversation.

After asking me where I grew up or chatting about the weather, they then sit back, turn on the video camera, and expect me to swiftly betray the superficial mood thus created by conjuring gut-wrenching tears suited for heavy dramatic material. This is akin to chitchatting with an Olympic sprinter at the starting line and expecting them to be in top form at the gunshot.

Similarly, I have walked into a few auditions for situation comedies where the environment was so cold and dour, that I half expected to see Sylvia Plath operating the video camera. Doing a sitcom audition with Sylvia makes it very difficult to channel one's inner clown, it would seem.

Of course, on an actual movie set, this lack of understanding of the acting process would never be tolerated. On set, everyone—from grips to costume people—appreciates that gabbing gleefully to an actor before a dramatic take distracts him or her from the work at hand. It is considered counterproductive to why we all are there.

There are, however, casting directors in New York and L.A. that understand the importance of treating auditions with the reverence afforded movie sets—these are the people who elevate the role of casting director to an art form and they are also the people who do the most interesting films and television. As I've become more and more bicoastal I've realized that famous line from the song "New York, New York" is completely untrue. If you can make it in *L.A.* you can make it anywhere. That line was true at the time the song was written, but one look at Broadway musical marquees and you will see a *Love Boat* lineup of L.A. TV actors slumming New York stages now.

Now, I am not suggesting that every dramatic audition be treated like a funeral procession. Nor am I suggesting that the Looney Tunes cartoon theme song blare on an endless loop at sitcom auditions. If only it were that simple. For there is another factor, besides tone, that stacks the odds against an actor excelling in auditions.

Most actors know that acting is ninety percent reacting and some casting directors, instead of hiring professional actors to "read" opposite you in an audition, instead supply non-actor "interns" or "assistants" to enact whatever love scene, dramatic confrontation, or comic repartee you have been called upon to perform that day. Or even worse, you have to actually read with the casting director themselves, with their face in the page, looking for their lines instead of watching your audition.

I have auditioned with some excellent readers opposite me who happened to be interns. But having the misfortune of auditioning with a casting intern who cannot act at all is very much like performing opposite a special effects "blue screen." I had this realization while auditioning for the film *Twister*, years ago in Oklahoma City. While standing in a tiny room with a video camera, I was asked to look at a stick the casting director held off-screen and react to it as if riddled with fear by a mammoth tornado bearing down upon me. I had some experience with twisters growing up in Texas and the sense memory of that kind of terror was as easy as putting on a hat.

"*Aaaahhhh!*" I screamed at the stick, eyes wide as saucers.

While this might seem silly and ridiculous, in that moment I realized that acting with a stick felt remarkably similar to some of the human casting interns I had read with over the years, some of whose amateurish line readings could make that stick resemble Lunt *and* Fontaine.

I didn't get one of the storm-chaser roles in *Twister* but I did learn an important lesson: If I was going to make it as an actor in Hollywood, I had better learn how to act with a stick, and with casting interns who act like sticks.

Now, I am a baby of indie films. That's where I've worked almost exclusively as an actor, and for good reason. Those films are closer to the films that made me want to be an actor in the first place.

Regardless of my indie background, there have been occasions when a film I am in has been "hot." During these brief windows of opportunity, I have made futile attempts at "crossing over" into more mainstream fare, usually while visiting the L.A. affiliate of my New York talent agents, people who did not sign me to work with their company but were contractually obligated to represent their New York office's clients when they were in town.

"He could play villains!"

"Yeah, can you do a Russian accent?"

"You're so dark! In a *good* way."

"So edgy—I mean, in a *good* way."

"Yeah, villains, definitely."

"Do you have a problem with mainstream movies?"

" 'Cause some of these indie actors are a little snobby!"

"Hahahaha!"

"Would you do TV?"

"Well, I'd rather just stick to movies."

"TV movies?"

"No, like good-quality movies. With good directors."

"Oh, I see."

"Well, then."

"I guess you don't like making money! Haha!"

"So you just wanna do indies? Don't you want a career?"

"We represent Fred Savage. He's doing indies now."

"And Alyssa Milano. She had a movie at Sundance last year."

"She's a great actress, people are gonna be shocked when they see her indie."

"Everyone wants a good indie now."

"Why not TV? I mean, nothing personal, but are you afraid to make money?"

"Are you afraid of success?"

"You really need to be on TV if you wanna get parts in indies nowadays."

"Harrison Ford just got an agent for the first time in his career—to help find him good indies."

"Indiana Jones is jonesing for an indie!"

"Craig cares about his work. Give him a break."

"Well, then, what about episodics?"

"A villain on *Touched by an Angel*!"

"There's always a villain on that show."

"Everyone watches that."

"What about sitcoms?"

"Can you be funny?"

"*Kiss Me, Guido* was funny."

"Would you be willing to bleach your hair again? Maybe that could be, like, your *trademark*."

"Gays and villains."

"Gay villains."

"Don't worry, we'll get you out there."

"We're like *this* with the New York office."

"One big happy family."

"Constantly in touch."

"Villians, definitely."

"Or sad guys."

"Sad gay villains."

"Perfect."

"Great."

"We'll get you out there for pilot season!"

"Nice to meet you, Craig."

Every spring, something magical happens in Los Angeles, called "pilot season." Pilot season consists of a three-month feeding frenzy where all the upcoming pilots for the fall TV season are cast. Most actors go West every year for this feeding frenzy, and at times I have been no different.

During pilot season, one is sent out on audition after audition, driving from one studio to the next, like some actorly treasure hunt in pursuit of a thirty-thousand-dollar-a-week paycheck. Because of the mass hysteria, it is common to go temporarily insane and find yourself salivating over the possibility of playing the kooky teacher in a spin-off of *Blossom*. Ready to sell your soul for that coveted role opposite "Urkel."

I have gone out on pilot season because I have at times gotten sick of making no money for my acting whatsoever.

My experiences with pilot seasons are somewhat of a blur, for it seems as though each audition was simply a carbon-copy repeat of others that preceded it, although some stand out more than others.

One fateful day, I received pages for a show that intrigued me very much. It was a one-hour drama for Warner Bros. Television; the name escapes me now—it was never picked up for airplay. The character I was up for was quite expertly written, complex and deep. Finally I felt I had found a TV pilot that would give me an opportunity to really act *and* make some money, pleasing my agents, my parents, and my empty belly.

In my audition scene, I was to be at a cemetery visiting the grave of my character's dead little brother. The monologue was very moving and sad and I was more than excited to have the opportunity to flesh it out at the audition.

When I arrived at Warner Bros. Casting, I waited nervously in the lobby, trying to conjure up the heavy emotions one might feel addressing the gravestone of one's dearly departed brother. I thought about people I had know who had died and remembered the times I had secretly spoken with them when no one else was looking.

After my name was called, I walked into the casting director's office. There, sitting behind a large desk, was a middle-aged, overweight man with what seemed to be a rather odd hair bun atop his round face.

"Hey. Ned. Casting director here."

"Hi, I'm Craig. Nice to meet you."

"Yeah, so how about this weather! Pretty nice, huh?"

Trying not to seem rude, yet determined to stay in my "depressed" state, I attempted a nod.

"Yeah, thank God I got the hell outta New York! Everyone's freezing their balls off right now! Sorry, suckas! Hahaha! You live here?"

"No—New York," I muttered.

"Oh well, get the hell outta there. No one casts outta New York anymore."

Upon closer examination I realized that his hair bun was actually an unbelievably long comb-over. From his right temple, I saw that he had grown out nearly a foot of his only available red hair and wound it about his head, like a frizzy red cinnamon bun.

"Yeah, New York's over. This is where it's happening!"

I looked at him, trying to remember that I was in a cemetery, not a casting office.

"Okay, let's get this over with! Gotta line out there a mile long!"

I took a moment to focus and do my best to remember my "dead brother."

As I began the monologue, I could tell that, despite the

distracting chitchat I had just endured (and expected), I had held onto my internal state of sadness. I ignored Ned and instead pretended that his desk was my dead brother's tombstone.

As the monologue continued, I felt increasingly morose. How could I go on in life without my little brother? My survivor's guilt was immense, my grief immeasurable. As I spoke to my baby brother, I could feel tears well up in my eyes. Ned and his cinnamon bun disappeared as the fluorescent lights were transformed into brilliant sunlight illuminating the graveyard in my mind's eye. I was crying now. But trying not to. I told my brother that I was sorry it hadn't been me. As I spoke, tears rolled down my cheeks. This was why I acted, to be able to—

"Ugh! I am so bored!"

Suddenly, I was snapped back to the room. I stopped talking and looked at Ned as he sat across from me, arms folded over his big belly.

"I am *sooooo* bored!" he moaned loudly.

I stared at him, my face wet from real tears.

"I'm bored after five minutes! You think people are gonna wanna watch this every week?" he snorted.

Shocked and suddenly *extremely* humiliated, I wiped the tears from my face and sat up. I know when I'm bad. I know when I'm phoning it in. I know when I'm believable. I was giving this fat man with cinnamon-bun hair gold!

Bolting up, I felt that side of me kick in, that part of me that's really a drag queen in disguise. Grabbing my "sides" I stormed to the door and opened it.

"How can someone who doesn't know good *hair* possibly know good *acting*!" I yelled at the top of my voice for all to hear. I slammed the door, ran to my rental car, and called my L.A. agent.

"Don't ever send me to that horrible man again!" I yelled.

After numerous, forgettable pilot seasons, I was finally forced to admit to myself that my aspirations as an actor do not lie in material I do not believe in. I simply cannot be good in projects I don't want to do because they are supposedly good career moves. I have arrived at this conclusion time and again, only to forget that truism about myself when my ego and pocketbook get involved.

My attempts to cross over in Hollywood have been akin to a huge movie star in Yugoslavia attempting to learn English and foolishly expecting the same success in America, when what he should have done all along is stay in Yugoslavia where what he does is appreciated.

Some may think that I am drunk with indignation on wine stomped from sour grapes, but my commitment to pursuing artistic fulfillment in my work rather than playing the kooky scientist on a WB TV show comes not from bitterness but lack of a certain kind of ambition.

I didn't put my finger on it until a few years ago while taking my dog, Baby, to a dog park in Silver Lake, near Los Angeles.

While standing and watching my dog run and play with other similarly frenzied mutts, I was approached by a man who worked for a film distribution company. I had met this man several times at the Sundance film festival, and we were chummy although I hadn't seen him in years.

"Hey! So, each year it seems I see you in yet another independent film. When are you going to do a real movie for a change? Aren't you just ready to fall off the tree, for God's sake?" he laughed.

I took a puff from my beloved cigarettes that I no longer smoke and turned to him and simply said: "I'm not ambitious in *that* way."

That was it. It was so simple yet I had not put it into such plain language before for myself or anyone else. I just wasn't ambitious in the way that an actor in Hollywood might be, the way, let's say, an actor like Kevin Spacey might be ambitious. I didn't pursue work that would make me famous. I pursued work that spoke to me, even if it was gay. Even if it was gay and indie and about gays who killed children or lesbians who shot famous artists. Even if it never played in a mall. Even if no one saw it but my friends. It occurred to me that I was living the career I secretly wanted in my heart, and that realization took away any feelings I might have had before about not being successful in a "Hollywood" way. My ambitions lay in doing good work, that's it. If I got the lead in the new Steven Spielberg movie it would be no different to me than working on *Swoon*, and that principle has enabled me to be honest about who I am and allowed me to do work that feels honest to me.

How one deals with rejection and insensitivity yet continues to remain an open and vulnerable person who cries in front of strangers is nothing less than miraculous and dumb and brave. Yet, for many actors, the maddening pursuit of fame can make them lose touch.

I don't buy into these books and programs that promise to crack the code of stardom for any actor. One of the biggest mistakes I see actors make is investing in hippy-dippy methods of attaining stardom as opposed to pounding the pavement or focusing on their craft. I have friends who spend hours writing in their wish journals, go to Artist Way classes, and chant every day, because they believe success is somehow divinely dispensed for good behavior and positive thinking. Santa has made his list of who's naughty and nice, but unfortunately, Santa, last I heard, is not in a position to cast NBC's new fall lineup.

It might disturb these spiritual barterers that most famous actors are not spiritual. For those who pray to God to be famous, who think that living a clean, good life is going to make you a star—any good biography of any celebrity will reveal that most stars have achieved their greatest success while either drunk, popping pills, sleeping with influential people, snorting drugs, or being a world-class asshole to all they encounter.

Personal happiness and talent are apples and oranges. Hopefully they can coexist but they are not mutually exclusive. History has shown that the most counterproductive barriers to true genius are a healthy childhood, healthy relationships, and healthy surroundings. If you have no demons to slay, then creativity becomes nothing more than a luxurious hobby motivated by vanity rather than the exorcising battle it was originally intended for. And then, of course, there's comedy.

Another disturbing aspect of being an actor is that you must be willing to live in a state of constant self-criticism and welcome the criticism of others. If you have a problem with being criticized, this is not the field for you. I have been told to my face by strangers that I was not talented, not attractive, and basically wholly unworthy of any accolades that might come my way. The most challenging aspect of being an actor is how to know when to listen to other people's criticisms and when to know it's projected horseshit.

During my last sabbatical to L.A. I decided to skip the agent thing and instead opt for a personal manager. An acting manager offers the kind of hands-on treatment usually not afforded at a large talent agency. The manager usually has fewer clients, is more picky about whom they represent, and thus more likely to "understand" the actor's vision of his or her career.

My first indication I had made a mistake in choosing my manager came fairly quickly. Upon meeting me, he made it a point that he had never taken on such an "interesting" actor as myself. Since he usually only represented model/actors, he had an unwavering conviction that I was hideously ugly—a fact, he warned me, would be a major obstacle in Hollywood.

I quickly found myself sitting in auditions surrounded by balding, troll-like character actors—competing for all the "kooky," ugly, and freakish parts in town. Whenever I would mention a role that I had heard about through friends, my manager would simply say, "No, they want someone okay-looking," or "They want someone handsome or cute." It didn't take me long working with him before I began to re-alize that my manager saw me as some kind of hideous beast.

Once I realized this, I fired my L.A. manager and, as I was picking up my headshots, he sighed and said, "Gee, I tried, Craig, but you're just not cute enough to work in L.A."

In the meantime, I continued to fly back to act in movies shot in New York, a city obviously in such throes of an ugly-actor shortage that they were willing to fly me, the Elephant Man, all the way across the country to be in their films.

Proving Martin Scorsese right, I've always gotten more act-ing work in New York than in Los Angeles, a city that I ac-tually love but that does not love me back enough to employ me.

When my indie film, *Kiss Me, Guido*, was bought by CBS to be turned into a sitcom pilot, my parents rejoiced. *This* would be it: Finally, Craig could make some money by reprising his role from the movie on the sitcom.

Kiss Me, Guido was meant to be a lark in an acting portfolio loaded with drama. Before *Kiss Me, Guido* came out, my image was so dour, audiences of mine half expected me to be at parties, in the corner, with a razor blade poised over my wrist. I would often disappoint those folks who had seen my films; they were expecting a brooding, tortured man, only to meet me and find a somewhat well-adjusted nice guy who actually likes making people laugh instead of wearing my anger on my sleeve.

In spite of my resistance to meeting with CBS to reprise my role in the *Guido* TV show, my agents and parents talked me into arranging a meeting. Secretly, I thought, the show was certain to be canceled pretty quickly and in the process I could pocket a little change.

"They changed your part. Now your character from the movie is morbidly obese," my manager groaned.

"Why?"

"There's already a funny slim white guy on *Will & Grace*."

"Is the character Frankie still a hot Italian guy?" I asked.

"Yeah, they got Danny Nucci."

I went on to ask my manager why it was thought of as okay to have more than one hunky Italian guy on television, but not more than one funny slim white gay guy?

Television has a long history in copying successful trends. But for the first time, it was not. Instead of "Rush out and get me the next Sean Hayes!" the opinion is, "Oh, there's already a Sean Hayes type on TV." I can't think of any other instance in television history when a successful trend was pointedly not copied.

My part, "Terry," was renamed "Vern" and was the only character from the movie to be radically changed in type. Eventually, he was not cast as a morbidly obese, self-deprecating gay man, but as a flamboyant Filipino.

The *Kiss Me, Guido* show was not a success, probably because it was retitled *Some of My Best Friends*. A writer on the show told me there was some talk in the beginning of calling it *Will & Won't*, since the producers were so terrified of the *Will & Grace* comparisons from the beginning. That the show was conceived around so much paranoia sucked any life out of what could have been a fun sitcom. That kind of panic never pays off creatively, because fear is anti-creative. And audiences can smell fear—especially if you're trying to make them laugh.

The day after the pilot premiered, I called my mom. She was still reeling with disappointment that I had not been on the show and raking in the big bucks.

"So, did you watch the *Kiss Me, Guido* TV show last night?" I asked over the phone.

"Oh, no! I most certainly did not!"

"Well, why not?"

"Because you're not on it, and I didn't want to give them any of my 'ratings'!"

"Mom, they don't know what you're watching."

"Huh? Oh yes they do. I have a cable box."

After explaining to my mother that there is a family called "the Nielsens," she seemed as if her entire world had been turned upside down. Then it all made sense. All these years, when I visited my parents, they seemed to be watching TV shows that I thought, knowing them, were strangely unsuitable to their tastes. British sitcoms, PBS, and The Weather

Channel were watched endlessly. Then I realized my parents thought that all of their viewing habits were being monitored and rated. They had been watching the less popular shows to give those struggling underdogs their "ratings." I loved them for that.

Smells Like Indie Spirit

"This is the most important haircut of my life," I carefully enunciated to the small Russian woman with the thick accent. I wasn't sure if she really believed me. I mean, if this *were* the most important haircut of a person's life, would he choose a Russian pink-and-black-lacquered beauty shop in Silverlake with faded nineteen-eighties posters of geometric works of hair art adorning the walls? Even the Russian lady knew she was at the bottom of the hair chain.

"Ten doller. You like shampoo, fifteen doller."

I quickly tabulated in my head the five-dollar difference and what it would do to my budget for that week.

"I'll take the fifteen-dollar one," I replied to her in very deliberate tones, so as to be fully understood. *Okay, so I'll smoke GHPs for a couple of days to make up the difference. The extra five bucks means I'm willing to splurge because, dammit, I'm worth it.*

I smiled a certain kind of pleading smile that begs for human connection. I remembered smiling that smile to a mugger once, praying he would recognize the humanity behind the wallet I was holding and not take my life. This time I pleaded for my hair.

Anyone who knows anything about the art of acting, knows that performing is ninety percent hair, five percent makeup, and five percent nepotism. Seeing that I had no relatives in the business, this increases my hair percentile to a full ninety-five. My future in show business was held in the scissors of a boxy Russian woman named Paulie.

Paulie stomped a cockroach and swung me around in the chair. She began yelling something in Russian to a small pretty woman whom I assumed was to give me five dollars' worth of shampoo and cranial massage. As I sat in the black-lacquered swivel seat, I looked in the mirror and thought: *Story of my life. Here I am up for an award in a few days and I have to get my hair cut in the cheapest salon in Silverlake.*

I had been nominated for Best Actor at the Spirit Awards, independent film's Oscar alternative, for my work in *Swoon*, which also happened to be my first film. I had made one thousand dollars on it, with no residuals since I was not in the Screen Actor's Guild at the time. The year between that paycheck and today had been long and, even though I cut corners, I went wild with the money and blew it on "non-essentials"—like food.

After a quick washing, worth all 500 cents, Paulie went to work as I sweated.

"You're actor. I can tell. Very vain. Insecure. Your hair is your 'instrument.' I know."

I nodded yes. *Oh my god, she's cutting off a lot*, I thought. But, to prove her wrong, I refused to buy into the stereo-typical "actorish" behavior she obviously expected of me, and assumed a cool, devil-may-care facade.

Snip snip. The struggle in me was great to maintain my composure while screaming, *"Watch what you're doing!"* on the inside.

"You have bad skin. No good. You need facial. Bill Campbell, he get facial, he care about his career. Not like you. Very bad."

Snip snip snip. More comes off. Another fantasy emerges. This time it's a newspaper headline: RUSSIAN HAIRDRESSER AND MOTHER OF EIGHT SURVIVES CHERNOBYL ONLY TO BE STABBED WITH OWN SCISSORS BY OPENLY GAY INDIE ACTOR.

"I do Bill Campbell's. He's 'Rocketeer.' He come in all the time for facial. You wait. You see. He gonna be big star." Paulie seemed obsessed with actor Bill Campbell, almost romantically. She was right too, he did achieve great success on television's *Once and Again*—certainly due to Paulie's exfoliating influences.

My back turned to the mirror, I could only imagine what was going on up there. When she turned me back around, I was not shocked so much by my botched, geometric haircut, as by my sheepish, haunted, glassy-eyed expression—like a Robert Downey Jr. mug shot.

I quickly paid Paulie, holding back the tears. My hair looked like an anvil. I could have pounded out horseshoes on it. I'd known that this could be a possibility when I sat in Paulie's chair, but prayed the gods would not go crazy on me. My hair was a casualty of my need to budget a celebrity's lifestyle on a temp worker's wages. I see bumper stickers that say POVERTY KILLS but what they really should say is POVERTY KILLS GLAMOUR. But—like most impoverished gay indie stars— I bucked up. I was already an hour late back from my lunch break.

I walked into my temp job at D.D.B. Needham, a large ad

agency, and sat down in front of my envelopes. Temping has always been my real career since I didn't start making good money as an actor until my seventh movie, *The Misadventures of Margaret*, which was only released in Europe. Before that, I had made a combined total of eighty-five hundred dollars on six movies, spaced out over seven years. In other words, $1,410 a year. Most of that money went into trips to Sundance, headshots, and to Uncle Sam.

It wasn't unusual for me to ask for time off from work to attend a premiere of a film I starred in or for an extended lunch break so that I could rush off to do a TV interview. There were film festivals, meetings, and Annie Leibovitz photo shoots to work into my schedule, and I needed job flexibility.

Unlike many actors, I have an utter inability to wait tables.

I had worked in a T.G.I. Fridays when I was fifteen as a busboy and was continually berated by my Dabney Colman look-a-like (and act-alike) manager for my complete lack of speed. I've always been easily intimidated by asshole-ish personalities and, since I am also afraid of confrontation, I told my manager and fellow T.G.I. employees that I was leaving my busboy job due to a recent diagnosis of leukemia. At fifteen, I had no idea what leukemia was; I just knew it was serious enough to quit a job cold turkey without showing up again. When I returned post-diagnosis to pick up my last paycheck, I was bombarded with hugs and tears from my fellow employees who damned a god that could condemn a lad so young as me to a terminal disease.

"Yeah," I said, not really knowing what symptoms I should be exhibiting, "I'm really tired all the time."

D.D.B. Needham had been a godsend. I had recently

moved to L.A. to pursue my budding acting career and needed money. I was making seven dollars an hour stuffing envelopes for the marketing campaign for *Jurassic Park* and worked alone in a cubicle with a clear view of my boss. Since I was obvious to everyone, I was constantly bombarded with friendship-seeking co-workers. I've always hated it when my temp-job co-workers tried to forge a relationship with me. I never want to feel too invested in my role as office peon. During that time, it wasn't uncommon for one of the secretaries to come running up to me, *Premiere* magazine in hand, exclaiming, "Isn't that you?" while holding up a picture of me in *Swoon*.

"Yeah," I would smile as I licked another envelope.

"You're in a magazine! What are you doin' here?"

"I'm doing research for a new film. It's about an underpaid envelope-stuffer who kills his nosy co-workers."

Just as I hit my full envelope-stuffing stride, I felt someone's eyes on me.

"What happened to your hair?" My boss stood before me, his glasses pulled down to study the sculpted black foam that Paulie had crafted.

He moved in closer as if observing a gruesome car crash. My hair was beauty-salon roadkill and he wanted to rubberneck.

"Oh, I got it cut." I tried in vain to deflate the anvil, flatten it.

"Well, I don't have to tell you that it's not exactly a professional 'look.' I mean, I know you're a musician—"

"I'm an actor," I whispered.

"—but this punky-funky thing isn't really appropriate for the office."

He waited for a response. I debated telling him that I had leukemia and would not return tomorrow except that I still didn't know what the symptoms are after all these years. Perhaps cancer of the hair. That would have been more believable, considering.

"I'll take care of it." *Stupid asshole. Don't you know who I think I am?*

"So, can you work over the weekend? The envelopes you stuffed are ready to be stamped and they need to go out first thing Monday morning."

"I can't. I have something I have to go to. An awards ceremony."

"Oh, really? What, the Oscars?" He laughed uproariously at the idea that an anvil-headed homosexual might acquire an invite to the upcoming Academy Awards.

"No, the Spirit Awards on Sunday. I'm nominated for Best Actor." There. I did it. I owned my shit and the cat was out of the bag.

"The 'Spirit Awards'? What is that, some New Age thing?"

"It's for independent films."

Nothing. He blinked.

"Like *sex, lies and videotape*?" I clarified.

My boss put his glasses back on his nose and headed towards his office.

"Okay, well, suit yourself. But it's time-and-a-half—ten-fifty an hour," he said, as only the man responsible for publicizing *Jurassic Park* could.

———

My mom had flown in from Texas the night before and was waiting for me at home. She had come to Los Angeles to accompany me to the awards ceremony, but mostly she came out to California to clean. My mother's capacity to clean makes Joan Crawford look like a lazybones; the second she gets in the door, she's off and running, with a kind of supernatural radar that detects dust bunnies otherwise naked to the human eye. When I got home, she was bleaching out my kitchen garbage pail in the sink.

"This garbage can is so dirty!" she chuckled. My mother chuckles about almost everything she says. She's a chuckler.

"That's because it's a garbage can."

"Whoo-ee, I'm dizzy from the fumes!" She chuckled herself into a chair to rest. Sweat poured off her brow, which she wiped off with the back of her rubber-gloved hand.

"Mom, why don't you rest? You just flew in," I moaned.

"I like cleaning your place. It makes me feel useful! Ooh, I love your haircut! It's neat!"

I went into the bathroom to wash Paulie and D.D.B. Needham right out of my hair. My mom knocked on the door.

"Oh, someone called for you! The head of NBC—or is that an *A*?"

I opened the door to the bathroom. "Pardon?"

"NBC or ABC casting. Oh, darn it! I can't read my own writing! He said he wants you to call him about coming in for an audition and that he's a friend."

"A 'friend' at *N* or *A*BC?"

"Well, I can't read my writing—I had these silly rubber gloves on when he called!" She chuckled, and off she went to reshingle the roof.

This had become a familiar situation for me lately. Because

of my Spirit Award nomination and the success of my first movie, everyone was suddenly calling me in for meetings. Normally an agent would field these offers and appointments, but my agents had dropped me only months before, and Fine Line, *Swoon*'s distributor, was forwarding any calls they received about me to my home number. Normally, the Screen Actor's Guild would have intervened in a situation like this. The only problem was that *Swoon* hadn't qualified me to join SAG, so I wasn't a member.

Right after *Swoon*'s premiere at the Sundance Film Festival, I was snapped up by a now defunct agency. This agency was a big deal in its day, but was bought out by a larger, more legendary, old-school talent agency. I went over to this agency with my agent, Paul, who was amazing but, regretfully, located in New York. I was told to go into the L.A. office to meet the new team of agents that would represent me. I drove down to Beverly Hills and entered the plush, vast offices.

While all the agents in an agency look to get you work, the "point person" is your main man. I was assigned to a man we'll call "Joe." I had experienced my share of "getting to know you"–type meetings before, but this one was different.

"Craig! Hey, I've heard great stuff about you, mister!" He motioned for me to sit down across from his desk. He picked up a pencil and fidgeted with it while we talked.

"So, how's L.A.? Think you're gonna stay?"

"Yeah, I want to see how things go," I mused. I could tell he was nervous. He seemed slightly flirtatious, too, which is par for the course in Hollywood, whether you're gay or straight, cute or ugly.

"So, you meeting people out here? Making friends?"

Joe was full of interest in me, but I almost felt like he was grilling me for some weird reason, digging for something.

When it comes to business, I like going into a meeting, doing the audition or reading, and leaving. But Joe wanted to *talk*.

We were bonding nicely. He gave me a conspiratorial look, then got up and closed the door to his office. He returned, and suddenly dropped his professional demeanor and a huge flaming queen emerged in its place. He started talking to me like a "girlfriend" and wanted to "dish."

"So, are you seeing anybody?" At this point, some kind of alarm went off in me. This seemed a little inappropriate. I couldn't put my finger on it, but I felt trepidation.

"Uh-huh," I said.

He jumped in. "I'm seeing this guy from San Francisco. Have you been up there? The guys are really hot. My boyfriend looks like Dean Cain."

I congratulated him on landing a beau and suddenly realized I had been in his office for an hour and a half and was feeling exhausted. He went on in detail about his love life, being gay and how gay people should stick together in Hollywood. He was so pro-gay I almost expected him to don Pride rings, start twirling a baton in the air, and break into a gleeful, leg-kicking rendition of "It's Raining Men." Caught up in this moment of sisterhood, I softened.

"I'm seeing this guy in Santa Fe. It's a long-distance thing, which is hard." I went on to elaborate how I seemed to function better in my life when I was in love and was more likely to do well in auditions because my entire source of approval wasn't coming from landing a job—trying to make this whole conversation relevant to why I was there.

"Well if he comes out, you can take him to some fancy Hollywood type functions."

"Oh, totally!" I smiled.

" 'Cause you're out of the closet in your career. Aren't you?"

"Well, yeah. I mean, it would be a little disingenuous if I wasn't, considering the movies I'm working in."

He suddenly got up and opened the door.

"Okay, well, great, Craig! I'm so excited to finally meet you! We'll get to work on getting you out there, pronto. You might wanna drop off more headshots and demo reels soon. Also, get me *Swoon* on tape—I know it's in the theaters but I never have time to actually go to the movies."

And I was off.

A few days later, my agent in New York called me.

"They don't want to represent you in L.A."

I was shocked. Everything seemed so great with Joe. We were "girlfriends"!

"Why? I don't understand."

"I don't know how to say this, but—you're gay. I mean, you're openly gay," Paul confided in me.

"I guess I'm also openly out of representation with a starring role in a movie coming out."

It was 1993 and the only other person who was "out" in the movie business was Harvey Fierstein, a lovable nonthreatening teddy bear whose roots were in Broadway.

Joe, like some gay men in Hollywood, had used his own gayness as bait to see how comfortable I was with my sexuality. He knew I was gay before I walked in. But what he didn't know, and wanted to find out, was how comfortable I was talking about it; whether I would be "political" or not. It's okay to be gay in show business—everyone is. You just can't talk about it, and if you do, you had better feel some trepidation, which I didn't. Not only that, but you'd better not do career-busting things like falling in love or taking a boyfriend to a premiere.

Swoon was in the theaters, I was receiving rave reviews, and I had no agent to help me capitalize on it. I can't imagine that any agent in their right mind would drop an actor at the very moment the actor's career exploded. I had a breakout role in *Swoon* and my agency dropped me because I was gay. If I had been straight, in a straight movie, playing a straight character, in a movie of *Swoon*'s caliber, I certainly would have had an agent that day the casting director from *A* or *NBC* called.

I called NBC and talked to the casting director. He was not a "friend," as my mother had noted, but was casting a show called *Friends* and wanted me to come in.

"We called your agents, but they didn't call us back!" he said.

"Well, I'm not with them anymore," I said, praying that he wouldn't see me as an agent-free loser, which in fact I was.

"Oh, well, we called them because of the *Reporter*."

"Huh?" I wondered aloud.

"The ad in the *Hollywood Reporter*, on the back cover?" he said innocently.

I rushed over to Book Soup, picked up an issue, and turned it over. There, in living color, was an expensive ad that read, "WE CONGRATULATE OUR SPIRIT AWARD NOMINEE: CRAIG CHES-TER," with the name of my former agency prominently displayed at the bottom.

My agents had dropped me and then patted themselves on the back for representing me the second I got an award nomination.

I found out later that NBC wasn't the only potential employer that had seen that ad and called my former agents to offer me work. They never forwarded the information to me and all those jobs "slipped through the cracks" forever. Paul and I remained friends, and the hideous dinosaur of an agency that he worked for eventually dropped him too.

After my mom had repaired my hair with her trusty scissors, we set off to find me something nice to wear to the awards. I was on a tight temp budget, so I had to be creative. As we sat in my Ford Taurus, my mom asked if there were any Wal-Marts in Hollywood.

"No. God—I wish I could get something at Barneys," I mused.

" 'Barneys'?"

"Yeah. The store. In Beverly Hills."

"They have a whole store for that purple dinosaur?"

The day of the awards came. I had found an outfit at a thrift shop, and my mom had dressed it up with new buttons she sewed on the night before. Mom put on her best Kathie Lee Gifford three-piece and we hit the freeway. Worried that bringing my mother would just be too Liberace, I asked my good friend Lisa LoCicero to join us as well.

Lisa was an actress and friend from New York who was gorgeous, sexy, and hysterically funny. We had met through a guy I had seen briefly in New York named Joel. Joel and Lisa had been scene partners in a theatrical showcase for agents, called *Excuse Me, but We're on Our Way to the Top!* Joel and I didn't work out, but I got custody of Lisa in the divorce so I was happy.

We picked up Lisa in Burbank. She was wearing a sexy, Goth-meets-dominatrix–type dress that looked like something you'd wear to audition as a backup dancer for Stevie Nicks. A choker of black velvet surrounded her neck and she looked hot.

After getting lost, and several four-letter words later, we arrived at the Spirit Awards, which were held under a tent on the beach on Santa Monica.

Now, Lisa and I had thought that this awards ceremony would be a polite little afternoon tea. I mean, these were awards for little independent films that most of America wouldn't see: this was before the Independent Film Channel or the Sundance Channel. When we showed up and saw that it was an absolute melee of stars and paparazzi, we panicked.

"Oh my god! This is huge!" Lisa observed.

My mom spotted Keanu Reeves in the parking lot.

"Oooo! Look, there's Christopher Reeve!"

After walking down the red carpet, with not so much as one photographer or reporter stopping to ask me what kind of tree I'd be, we took our seats at the Fine Line Features table. Sitting next to me was the also-nominated director of *Swoon*, the genius Tom Kalin, and the film's brilliant director of photography, Ellen Kuras, who was also up for an award. Robert Altman sat next to my mom—who had already whipped out the video camera and was shooting footage of the many celebrities, none of whose names she could place.

"Oh, what was he in?" she wondered as she taped Billy Baldwin. "*Red November? Hunting for the Red November*, that's it!"

The videotape of my mother's day at the Spirit Awards is something to behold. There are images of Miranda Richardson, Jeff Goldblum, Laura Dern, and Andie MacDowell staring into the lens with an expression that can only be interpreted as *Who is this lady in the peach, turquoise, and purple outfit blatantly filming me from ten feet away?*

My mother settled the camera on a blonde Kelly Lynch.

"Ooo, I love her! Daryl Hannah!"

The awards were nerve-racking. There were huge projection screens that loomed on both sides of the stage, so the audience could see clips of the nominees' work.

The whole day passed rather slowly and surreally during the luncheon and dinner. I noticed that my mom seemed preoccupied with Robert Altman and every time I checked up on her she was asking him very specific questions about the meal we had been served.

"How would you cook this chicken? Sauté it? Grill it?" He would then respond by going into minute detail of how he would have prepared the standard-issue catered chicken breast with asparagus. I was relieved. *Good, thank God—he can keep her busy while I get properly drunk.*

Being that the bar was open and everyone in showbiz, myself included, is um, "very thirsty," the lines to the bathrooms were where the action was. While standing in line, Steve Buscemi exited a stall and ran right into me.

Steve and I had worked together a few years before on a short film with Amanda Plummer. In it, I played—believe it or not—the ghost of his high-school football coach. I was obviously cast before people saw me only as "that gay guy."

While Steve was congratulating me on *Swoon*'s success, Harvey Keitel came up and interrupted us, hugging Steve.

Keitel had been nominated for *Bad Lieutenant*, in which he was brilliant playing a junkie cop who trades his immortal soul to feed his addictions. As I watched him talk to Steve, I couldn't help but think about his performance and how, if I ever played roles like that, but gay, I would be criticized for portraying a "negative role model." If a straight man plays a fucked-up drug-addled sex addict, he's "brave" and his work takes center stage and he doesn't have people telling him he can't do complex roles for fear of making straight men look bad.

Steve turned Harvey around and introduced me to him. Harvey acted like no one had told him he was competing with other actors that day.

"Huh?" he wondered as he looked at me.

"Harvey, this is Craig." Steve motioned; Harvey drew a blank. "He's competing with you today," Steve reminded him.

Harvey Keitel looked at the ground, shook my hand.

"Oh! Good to meet you, Fred! I wish you the worst of luck!" he joked.

Miranda Richardson announced the nominees in my category. I was terrified, not because of the awards but because I think Miranda Richardson is a genius and I was overwhelmed at potentially having to go up onstage and meet her. She said my name and everyone in the tent put down their forks, turning to the big-screen TVs. There, a clip of my work in *Swoon* began flickering. I noticed Jodie Foster, Neil Jordan, and Alfre Woodard turn to watch me on the big screens. *This is so not happening. There's been some kind of mistake!* I fantasized about running up and unplugging the TVs—"Just kidding!"

I didn't win the award, of course, knew I wouldn't, and was secretly relieved. Really.

We left the awards dazed. I had spent my whole life watching some of these very people in mall theaters in Texas when I had wanted nothing more than to work in movies.

The first movie I ever saw was *The Sound of Music* at the Cinerama Dome Theater in L.A. I was only a few months old, but even at that noisy age my reverence for movies was firmly entrenched. My mom claims that, unlike most squealing bundles of joy, the movies were the only place she could take me where I *wouldn't* scream my head off. As I hit puberty and had the lucky realization that I was pretty much doomed to glory holes and show tunes for the rest of my life, I masochistically sought out those movies that offered me a catharsis. At my eleventh screening of *Sophie's Choice* in high school, I realized why the movies were for me. I loved feeling sad. I loved the blues. I had found my savior and her name was Mary Louise Streep.

Yet while my mom knew I was in love with the movies, she was in love with her children and wanted security for me. Things like awards didn't impress her much. She had spent the whole day swapping recipes with Robert Altman—one of the most brilliant directors of our time—and could have cared less how he made his living. She judged a person on how nice he or she was, how open.

After the awards, we drove my mother home. Actress Catherine Keener had invited Lisa and me to Melissa Etheridge's house for an intimate post-awards soirée.

"I wish you would move back home," my mom said. "I don't like you living here, what with all the earthquakes."

She knew I had big dreams, that I loved movies and loved acting. My career made my mom uncontrollably worried. My career took me away from her.

"And there's a fault line that runs right through Manhattan. I read about it in the *Weekly World News*. It's dangerous in New York, too!" she warned. "Just not safe."

"Mom, in the one week I visited you last year, a tornado

hit our house. A couple of days later, two twin engine planes collided over our front yard and set the neighborhood on fire. There were body parts on our lawn. Remember?"

"Well, I just think you should come back home and give up this acting thing. You've never made any money at it."

"You just went to an awards ceremony where your son was nominated for his acting work. Don't you think that means I might actually have a chance at doing this for a living?"

"They shoot lots of movies in Dallas!" she chuckled.

"Mom, the only thing that's been shot in Dallas is Kennedy."

"No, they filmed *Tender Mercies* there. And *Robocop*. The TV show, *Dallas*, of course, and—"

She took a gulp of iced tea and paused. Should she pull out the heavy artillery? This awards thing was going to be tough. This awards thing could keep him in this crazy business for another ten years alone.

"*Silkwood*," she mumbled, almost afraid to look up to see my reaction.

She knew how I felt about Meryl. How dare she play the Meryl card. Wow, she must be desperate!

"Meryl Streep lives in Connecticut, Mom. Just because she did *Silkwood* in Texas is neither here nor there. It's called being 'on location.' "

"I read that she was spotted at Six Flags with Cher while they were filming in Fort Worth!"

"And?"

"Well, I'm just saying, you never know where you might get discovered! There are big stars working in Dallas now and they're out and about—"

"Are you implying that I should move back to Texas, hang out in amusement parks, pray that Meryl Streep does another movie in Dallas, and one day, after she gets a hankerin' to ride bumper cars with Cher, goes back to Six Flags, upon which she spots the obvious acting talent oozing from every pore of my body, and immediately hires me to be in her next movie?"

"Well, no! Don't be smart. I know how it works. You'd have to audition for her first."

I dropped my mom off at my house and went inside so that Lisa and I could freshen up for Melissa's party. My mom immediately went to the phone to call my dad and "check in."

She began to relate the many star sightings she had witnessed to my dad.

"Well, guess who I sat next to today?" she told him. "The Frugal Gourmet!"

I looked at her as I took off my shoes.

"Mom, that was Robert Altman!"

She cupped her hand over the phone.

"Who?"

My mother had been asking Robert Altman all day for his expert advice on food preparation. I don't know if he knew this Texas housewife was mistaking him for TV's lovable chef, but apparently, from what I overheard at least, he makes a mean chicken cacciatore.

Lisa and I drove up to Melissa's house in the Hollywood Hills, which was situated at the top of a ridiculously steep driveway. Lisa and I were nervous. The day had been so exhausting and here we had to sparkle all over again.

We parked at the bottom of the hill and grunted our way to the top of what seemed to be the steepest driveway ever. After ringing the doorbell, a dog began barking inside. The door flew open.

"Hi!" Melissa Etheridge stood before us. She was tousled

in that sexy earth mother way and was attempting to hold back a huge black lab that zeroed in on my crotch as if my privates were made of pork rinds.

"Sorry! God, she must really like you!" Melissa grunted as she tried to restrain the groin-fixated pooch. I appreciated her trying to smooth this event over, but I started to feel a tad bit self conscious—especially when the entire room of guests craned to check out my package.

The dog suddenly lost interest in my nuts and ran off happily, knocking over lamps and knick knacks while Melissa did her best to sweep up behind the bull in her china shop. Julie Cypher took over and stepped in as host. I could immediately tell that she and Melissa were a couple and were in love.

"Hi! I'm Julie. Come on in. That's so weird. Do you have a cat or something?"

"Yeah," I smiled. I wanted to make a joke about unzipping my fly to show her my pussy, but I have wisely learned to reserve my crass and tasteless sense of humor for the displeasure of only my closest friends.

After introducing ourselves, Lisa and I entered the cabin-like living room. There was a fire in the fireplace and it was all very cozy shabby chic.

Lisa and I got a glass of wine and mingled in the living room. The party was small, maybe ten people, including Dermot Mulroney and his wife Catherine Keener, who was up for Best Actress that day for her work in *Johnny Suede*. This gathering was in her honor and we commiserated over glasses of Merlot.

I refilled my glass and went to the roaring fire, kneeling down to get warm. A blonde woman was sitting at the hearth cross-legged.

"Recovered from Cujo the crotch sniffer?" she joked.

"Yeah, I guess he likes Vienna sausage," I joked. *Joked*. It is a known fact that only men with unbearably large penises feel confident enough to joke about having a tiny penis. So there.

The blonde woman laughed.

"I'm Ellen."

I introduced myself.

"So, did you go to the awards today?" she asked, leaning back on the palms of her hands.

"Ugh. Yeah. I lost to Harvey Keitel."

"Well, it's cool you got nominated. Although I'd love to see someone at an awards ceremony be honest when they lose. Like jump up from their seat and storm out of the Dorothy Chandler Pavilion crying."

I started to laugh. "Totally. I know!" I shot her a "you're funny" look and arched my eyebrows.

"I do stand-up," she remarked.

"That's funny because you're the only one sitting at the party," I said.

Ellen was shy and sweet—not the kind of person you would expect to be a stand-up comedienne. Her blonde hair was long and she seemed like a lesbian Princess Diana.

Later, I sat on the couch, slightly buzzed, talking about this and that with my hosts.

"What's it been like being in a gay movie?" asked Julie.

"We're not supposed to call it a gay movie according to the distributors," I moaned.

Everyone laughed and moaned.

"So, are you out?"

"Um." It was still hard for me to own being gay at that point. I was still scared of whether people would judge me or think I was a political gay radical. When you're an actor, the need to be liked is immense. Being openly gay sort of flies in the face of that actorly need. "Yeah. I'm out. I've been out since the movie premiered at Sundance."

Ellen, Melissa, Julie, and I sat on their couch and, while Melissa strummed her guitar, I told them about my experiences up to that day with homophobia in Hollywood, complete with my agents dropping me right as my big starring vehicle opened. I left nothing out: I had been called a fag to my face on the set by an assistant director, been told I was either too gay or not gay enough to play any mainstream gay roles, had countless people in power ask me "why can't you just be an actor—why do you have to be a gay actor?," had a gay therapist tell me that being openly gay in Hollywood was a form of self-destructive behavior as opposed to something to be proud of and lauded for. The stories seemed endless.

"I guess I don't make being out sound so hot," I realized. At the time, I couldn't think of many positive aspects of what I was doing. At the time it basically just sucked and was scary because I was twenty-five and had no one to look up to, to see how they survived being an openly gay movie actor.

Years later, when Ellen came out on her TV show and made history, I cheered. I felt the same way when Melissa came out. I wasn't anybody important. I had no voice—I was not a celebrity yet was out from the beginning. Coming out in the beginning of your career is like finishing the race before the bleachers are even assembled. There's none of that juicy speculation of "is he or isn't he" or gossip like "he slept with the brother of my cousin's ex-boss." Being out in the beginning takes the fun out of it for everyone else but you. So much has changed since but its baby steps. After Ellen, I hoped there would be an avalanche of closeted actors coming out. There wasn't. The closet just got more sophisticated and guarded by lawyers.

Now when Ellen or Melissa says there's homophobia in Hollywood, people listen. When I pointed these things out, people had the prerogative of saying, "he's paranoid" or "making things up." Now, with celebrities coming out and saying the very things I said privately for years, people have realized I'm not just overly sensitive or into being a victim.

"Oh my god. Oh god," Lisa whispered to me in a conspiratorial tone.

"What?" I asked.

"Look who's out by the pool," she whispered, indicating a window that peered out into Melissa and Julie's backyard. There, sitting in a lounge chair, was Brad Pitt. He had been banished to the backyard, being the only smoker in the bunch besides myself.

I had met Brad several times, both at Sundance and through a mutual friend of ours, Yoram Mandel. To me, he was just this nice guy from Missouri but to Lisa—well, she's a straight woman and he's Brad Pitt.

"Go talk to him," I suggested. "He's nice."

Lisa rejected that notion. She was too shy. But I wasn't. I wanted a cigarette.

I moved outside and asked for a light. He jerked to life and lit me. I sat across from him on the end of another lounge chair. Brad had been a presenter that day and knew I had lost.

"Sorry you didn't win."

"Oh, thanks."

I took a long, much-needed drag. It was the perfect temperature to smoke—around fifty-eight degrees.

"It's so weird. Tomorrow I have to go back to my job stuffing envelopes for seven dollars an hour."

Brad looked at me and grinned in disbelief.

"I know. I just wish—today was so heady and so unreal because it's like I'm two people. The actor and the temp. One day I'm having Robert Altman telling me what a fantastic actor I am, and the next day I'm licking envelopes."

We sat and smoked.

"I just wish I could make a living at it—like you do."

Brad blew a smoke ring and turned to me.

"You know what?" he said, lying back in the lounge chair. "I wish I was nominated for an award."

Brad and I went inside and we all sat around while Melissa played requests on her guitar. We sang "Delta Dawn, What's That Flower You Got On" and other classics. I had finally found the gay version of church camp that I had been looking for my whole life.

Lisa and I stumbled out of the party late into the night. It had rained and the scary hill down to the car was slippery and wet. We carefully made our way down when, suddenly, we heard someone say "Good night!"

It was Brad, who was out front now, smoking yet again. His salutation startled Lisa and she slipped, sliding down the hill, feet first. A few days before, Lisa and I had gone to J.C. Penney's so that she could buy a thong for her Stevie Nicks chiffon outfit. Brad and I watched, horrified, as her new black thong bikini shined in a street lamp's glow, skirt up over her head, while she screamed and wrestled her way down the never-ending slope. I ran down afterwards. She was nervously laughing when I got to her and I helped her up.

"You okay?" Brad asked.

The most embarrassing thing that could ever happen to a straight woman had just happened to Lisa—she had made a fool of herself in front of the Sexiest Man Alive. I grabbed her hand and we ran to my car, laughing and hooting it up the whole way.

Chesters Roasting on an Open Fire

Despite having left the Lone Star State forever, there are certain occasions at which I am contractually obligated to show my face at the Chester manse. Typically, my contractual obligations have been met by my annual Christmas trip.

Every Christmas is met with long-established traditions. Every year I get the same things—slippers, a Scorpio horoscope calendar, socks, and underwear.

The reason we get the same thing every year is because everything we received the previous year came from discount chains and has broken or fallen apart due to poor manufacturing.

My mother, upon the mere site of a Wal-Mart store, has been known to fall into the dead-eyed abstraction usually reserved for crack-cocaine addicts and lifetime-achievement-award recipients. The scene is always the same.

As we pull up into the Wal-Mart parking lot in her champagne-colored Cadillac, beads of sweat begin to form on her upper lip. My mother must have painted HANDICAPPED

PARKING signs in a past life, because she has the most amazing parking karma, without fail. Her hands begin to shake as she puts the car in park. Purse in hand, the struggle within her to resist sprinting for the doors is great. Before I know, it, we are inside and are met by a "Greeter," usually a senior citizen or handicapped person, who wills us to "have a nice day," something that Linda can't not do if she's at her beloved Wal-Mart.

There I will get the same things I got for everyone the year before. Noticing how a product has improved or changed in a whole year is the usual topic of conversation while we shop and is always met with, "Why did they have to go on and change that?"

The thing that my mother annually receives is not found at Wal-Mart. It's a little too fancy for that. And in Texas, "fancy" is French for "real nice."

Every year my mom receives a porcelain doll from me. Outfitted in old-fashioned Victorian and Edwardian garb, as if the happy result of a QVC archaeological dig, Jennifer, Brittany, Charlotte, and Lindsey's lifeless bodies are frozen in timeless childhood innocence. Peeking out of glass–and–faux wood tombs scattered throughout our house, my mom's little porcelain prisoners never age, never hit puberty, and never leave home. Jennifer could never pursue acting; Brittany could never eat a grown man's ass; Charlotte can't ever talk back. The most action they ever see is the occasional feather duster.

My dad unwraps something gadgety—like an alarm clock with "soothing" nature sounds. It's amazing how similar rain and wind can sound when emitted from a microchip. If it's not a soothing-sounds clock, it's some Brookstone device that gives middle-aged men the five-minute illusion of being a suburban James Bond.

Our Christmases are ridiculously excessive. My dad has spent most of his life trying to provide for the family, and works his butt off. He is the hardest working man I have ever met and I literally watched his butt whittle away as he worked. Now it's gone completely. Just a set of love handles with two legs growing out of them.

Another familiar theme to Christmas at the Chesters' seems to be the nearly endless parade of future ex-boyfriends of mine. Just when my family has relaxed into believing that I have finally found someone dumb enough to love me, that person gives me the boot. My bringing men home seems to have become almost a holiday tradition. Each year I would bring in a new "guest star" and my family would laugh at his jokes, buy him gifts, and listen to his dreams and problems, while valiantly pretending that this had not happened the year before with an entirely different boyfriend all together. My parents have now evolved so much as human beings that they have come to embrace my gay "lifestyle" more than I have, the "lifestyle" of which I assume to be that of career bachelor.

Being a romantic and also being a gay man is like being a celebrity who shuns the spotlight. People think, "What is wrong with him? He's getting all this action and yet he complains." When you are a gay romantic, people tend to see you as weak or having bought into some dying ideals of romanticism, riding a dinosaur instead of taking a cab to meet your friends at the gay bars. There the dinosaur sits, waiting patiently outside of Wonderbar or Beige or Barrage, ready to take you home at 4 A.M., alone as usual, or to have sex with someone who doesn't like dinosaurs at all. You will be told to lighten up, or that it's just in man's nature to want to get their holes filled as much as possible. You will listen, and nod, and have lots of sex as they say you are biologically entitled to, and in your private moments know that it is all bullshit but you think, *I am gay and this is what gays do*. Or you grow up and realize that gays may do what they do and that's just swell, but that you are more than just a gay with a hole. You have a name and you'd like someone to use it with tenderness once in a while.

At home, my name is used with tenderness. It is lovingly adorned on my Christmas stocking, painted in glitter and glue, to remind me of who I am and from whence I came. Christmas morning it will be overflowing with millions of little factory-made oddities that you can't believe someone actually makes their living manufacturing. Going through them I can also find candy I will not eat and Christmas-themed pencils that I will never use but feel too guilty to throw away.

During a recent trip home, I decided to help my mother and father create the Winter Wonderland that their home becomes at the holidays—a monumental task of backbreaking proportions.

As you enter the foyer of our ranch-style Texan house, you will be greeted ceremoniously by a strange animatronic child holding a fake candle and moving in a circular fashion, as if slowly indicating, "Welcome to my world." Since the advent of home animatronics, there is constant movement of lifeless Christmas bodies near every wall socket—my mother's dolls come to repetitive life. My parents' house is so excessively decorated at Christmas it at times can resemble the "It's a Small World" ride at Disneyland. But rather than representing the many nations and ethnicities of the world, these gliding limbs and rolling heads hail straight from the North Pole.

Several hundred hours later, the Christmas decorations will

be finished and we will all sit and marvel at the grandiosity of our achievement. Lights will twinkle off shredded aluminum of every conceivable color, creating the illusion of an elfin discotheque. As a respectful nod to our Irish roots my mom will make her traditional Irish coffee, but I won't drink much because I will certainly already be high on the Vicodin I have secretly stolen from her medicine cabinet.

On Christmas Eve, we will drive to my cousin Cherry's trailer park just outside of San Antonio. We will talk about how much we miss going to my Aunt Carol's trailer park near Dallas, and how much we miss our other cousins Shandra and Angela who live there as well. But now we live in San Antonio and our only relative is Cherry.

There we will sit with my cousin and her many illegitimate children and pretend to enjoy ourselves until someone has the nerve to suggest leaving or pretends to suddenly have a stomachache. Illnesses are valid reasons to exit a situation at my cousin Cherry's house; anything less than physical pain, like being tired or ready for bed, is considered an insult. When my mother, father, sister, and I enter the world of my extended family, the rules change almost immediately. There, one shows their love not by giving gifts or compliments but by suffering or sacrificing one's own happiness or desires.

The only thing worse than foisting my own co-dependent, doomed love relationships onto my family is having theirs foisted onto me. Since all my cousins are straight women who live in trailer parks in Texas, they date straight men who also live in trailer parks in Texas. Usually, these amorous intrigues are unaccustomed to my refined and somewhat confusing ways.

One recent Christmas Eve, I was treated to the pleasure of

meeting my cousin Cherry's new beau, a mechanic named Vernon. Vernon was aggressively macho. He made Patton look like a geisha.

"Where ya from that ya dress that way?" he asked, remarking on my smart Christmas outfit, which consisted of a white button-down shirt, tie, and green-and-red plaid vest.

"I live in New York City."

"Ain't you scared of the AIDS there?" he farted.

Cherry dated very macho men because she herself was the most masculine straight woman I had ever met. Each time I would see her, she would use our time together as a sort of primal therapy session in gay bashing, all shrouded in the veil of bombastic humor.

Vern and Cherry both possessed the kind of destructive machismo that has been responsible for pretty much all oppression and misery on this planet. I tried to fool myself into thinking that it was different with Cherry because she was a woman, but I was wrong. The genitalia don't really signify when a person is an asshole. All the teasing I got from Vernon about being a fag I also got from the masculinely superior Cherry, who used these Christmas Eve get-togethers as opportunities to embarrass me in front of her friends and my family.

"Hey, everywun! Did ya'll see *Kiss Me, Guido*?" she hollered, fully done up in ten-gallon hat, bolo tie, and tuxedo. "My cousin Craig wuz the eeefiminut gah with blohn har!"

She then launched into an embarrassing (and shockingly untrue) imitation of me as "Terry" in *Kiss Me, Guido*, attempting to act "eeefeminate" which, for Cherry, comes about as easily as a frigid preacher's wife. She pranced around like a limp-wristed pansy, much to the belly-laughing delight of her other macho friends, male and female alike. I suddenly felt as if I had been magically transported back to the locker room in high school. I wondered if being teased for being femmy is okay if a non-femmy female does it. One look at Cherry's overwhelming inability to imitate an effeminate man imitating an effeminate woman and I realized that she had long ago copped to America's winning team of masculinity. I was still on the losing team of feminine virtues, of the sensitive sissy. There is nothing to gain when a woman makes fun of you for being gay. At least when a straight guy does it, there's a chance he'll throw you down and make passionate love to you. Any time I noted that Cherry had evolved into a macho bully, my parents would just nod their heads and say, "Well, you feel this way cause you have a problem with rejection. If a bully beat you up at school, you always took it personally."

"Uh—yeah!"

When I was growing up I was either harassed or beaten up nearly every day of my life. Lunch, recess, breaks between classes, pep rallies, these were simply opportunities for bullies to practice their butt-kicking skills on me unfettered by the probing eyes of school staff. There were times when the abuse from other boys was so heinous that my parents would be called up to school to intervene, as if I was somehow responsible for my battery. Graduation for me was akin to being liberated from some kind of horrible, thirteen-year boxing match.

My defense in situations with bullies has always been my brain and a somewhat iffy ability to qualify human behavior. I would quietly sit back and analyze Cherry, wondering where she was "damaged" or who had given her the "issues" that obviously kept her from realizing her full potential by becoming a bitch. Instead of confronting her and standing up for myself, I tried being compassionate towards her mean ways and boorish demeanor. It probably isn't a coincidence that all of the people that I know who preach compassion are also the people I know who are terrified of confrontation. It seems to me that the patronizing nature of compassion can be a hell of a lot easier than having to confront an asshole. Compassion is essentially passive and can be done privately, while gardening perhaps. Confronting an issue or person means forcing yourself to grow up, be a man. For people afraid of confrontation, "compassion" can be a marvelous scapegoat—you get to remain fearful of others and have the added bonus of feeling spiritually superior to them at the same time.

So I sat back and thought, *How sad for her, for all bullies. They just didn't get the love they should have had as children*. The thing I didn't learn until later in life is that most bullies quite enjoy being bullies and that assholes do not think of themselves as assholes. In fact they probably think that you're the asshole and to justify their bad behavior, they will suggest that you are "overly sensitive." Thinking someone is "overly sensitive" is the telltale remark of an asshole's denial.

After we left Cherry's we drove home, exhausted from the strain of pretending to be clueless and interested in Cherry's life.

There's an unknown flip side to the warm glowy womb of Christmas Eve. And that is you really are quite vulnerable. Everyone's guard is down that night.

Once ensconced in the mutually supportive home of my immediate family, I got into my pajamas. I do not wear pajamas in my real life in New York. I sleep in the nude. But there is something about sleeping in the nude at one's parents' house that feels slightly obscene. When I am home, I am smooth "down there" like a Ken doll and have no sexuality whatsoever except in theory.

My mother unwrapped the one gift that Cherry had given us but hours before—a basket of pinecones with two candles protruding upwards. A small song sheet of Christmas music fit between the two candles.

My mother looked for a place to set down Cherry's decoration. I have always thought it strange to receive a holiday decorative item as an actual holiday gift. It seems a little useless at any other time of the year and probably has more to do with the gift giver's holiday spirit while purchasing it than any kind of altruistic consideration of the recipient. Nestled into a small crevice next to an animatronic Mrs. Claus, my mother lit the candles and went to the kitchen to make pies.

An hour later, I decided to unwind by laying in front of the television on my stomach with the screen a foot away from my face as I had done when I was a child.

On cable TV there was a gruesome movie unfolding in which a woman was being hung nude and set ablaze with some kind of sticky fiery napalm. Lying on my stomach I began to realize how truly impressive my parents' new big screen television was. It literally overpowered the already overpowering room full of Christmas decorations.

The sound on this new television is so amazing, I thought. *Surely it has to be Dolby Surround sound or some kind of THX stereo*. I watched the nude woman aflame, horrified and perturbed at how violent movies have become. The camera moved in and I watched burning boobs on my parents' super-duper boob tube.

"Oh my god! Craig!"

My mother's screams produced a kind of jolting, immediate terror in me and I turned around to face a now flaming Mrs. Claus animatronic. Mrs. Claus's sweeping gestures took on an almost demonic nature as she gyrated and beckoned while engulfed in fire. Behind her was the source of the rapidly growing inferno—the basket of pinecones Cherry had given us had been set ablaze by the shrinking candles my mother lit hours earlier.

My mother entered the living room and desperately grabbed the nearest, largest item to extinguish the fire: a large stuffed Santa Claus doll. Santa Claus began beating Mrs. Claus with all my mother's might. The basket containing the pinecones had disintegrated, sending each and every pinecone on a personal mission to wreak individual havoc on our home. Very soon, there were ten little fires going at once.

My sister, who had a broken leg at the time, hobbled into the room without her crutches, screaming at what she was encountering—our Winter Wonderland was beginning to resemble the fiery pits of Hell. Tinsel burned and melted, fake snow under the tree went up like a book of matches. I desperately chased the fire around the room, grabbing whatever I could to put out the emerging flames. My sister, who was now crawling on the floor, dragged her leg cast behind her and was squirting tiny flames in the shag carpeting with a water bottle, with even more water bursting from her frightened eyes.

"Throw it outside!" my mom screamed as Santa beat the flames off his wife, who was now resembling the skeleton of a robot—a tiny "Terminator" with a hair bun and spectacles. "Throw the fire outside!"

With that, we threw the fire outside. I have no idea how we did it, but the fire that was in our living room was now on our front lawn. Everything in our living room was in some stage of combustion and, with the aid of oven mitts, my mom and I threw it all out: furniture, a rack of smoldering coats, lamps, my mother's grandfather clock, flaming boxes, singed animatronics, everything went out that front door—even the Christmas tree.

My father, who had run up to 7-Eleven to get my mom some vanilla, drove up to his house, only to discover that the contents of his house were now on the front lawn, blazing like a fiery art instillation.

My father ran into the house as smoke billowed out the door at him. There he found my sister, my mother, and I in the middle of the living room, covered in soot, holding each other. It was all gone. All our decorations, all our presents. The carpet was half melted; the wallpaper was peeling itself off the wall. My father came over and we four hugged each other, crying at losing our beloved decorations. For years I had secretly rolled my eyes at the excessive commercialization that had come to embody my parents' house during this time of the year. But now it was all gone. I looked around me, at the charred expanse of what, just moments before, had been a kind of theatrical ode to my mother and father's enthusiasm and I realized that it wasn't commercialism that went up in smoke, it was my parents' generosity of spirit, of their creativity expressing itself once a year in these decorations. The tears on their faces said it all. We all looked like scared children even though we weren't.

The night of the fire I re-discovered my love for my family, and I thought perhaps this is why fires exist. I had always taken these decorations and little people in motion for granted. But I had not seen the forest for the flaming Christmas trees.

15

Calling All Angles

As my boyfriend's best friend washed the dishes in my Los Angeles apartment, it occured to me that "generosity" can often be used as a form of control.

Nancy was a performance artist in Los Angeles whose "art" consisted of masturbating with fruit on stage for up to an hour, achieving orgasm, then cutting up the fruit and serving it to the less-than-enthusiastic audience.

Now, I don't even like fruit, let alone when its been rubbed up against my boyfriend's best friend's clitoris for an hour. Nor do I need to wait an hour for a performer to have an orgasm. I expect more efficiency and professionalism than that when I go to the theater. As I sat in the dilapidated theater watching Nancy moan and groan, all I could do was think, *If I was the star of the show, it would all be over barely before the curtain came up and everyone could eat the fruit before it ever had a chance to get into my ass and we could all go home with plenty of time to catch back-to-back* Golden Girls *reruns on Lifetime.*

As Nancy went about the kitchen, she began suggestively picking at a half-eaten bowl of fruit salad on the counter, as if lost in a sense memory.

Her friend Kenny and I had been together for nearly two years and were about to leave our dishwasher-equipped Hollywood apartment for a Hell's Kitchen tenement that didn't even have a sink in the bathroom.

Moments before, Kenny had told his lady friend of our imminent departure. Suddenly, her "abandonment issues" came roaring to the surface. "I hate you for taking my spiritual brother away from me!" she laughed in a way that is actually not laughter.

"I'm not taking Kenny away, Nancy! He's a thirty-two-year-old man! I think he's old enough to make his own decisions."

"Kenny is in A.A. and New York is a town of drinkers. His recovery should be the most important thing to him. Not your relationship."

When someone qualifies your love as a hindrance to their friend's recovery, to his very well-being, how can you possibly defend your right to be in his life? To Nancy and many others, a wartime mentality exists in recovery that supercedes honoring love, loyalties, or commitments. In the name of sobriety, inconsequential things like lovers or families pale in comparison.

Nancy had spent many, many years in support groups of one kind or another. In her mind, it was absolutely impossible to solve one's problems without them.

Nancy was a New Age overachiever. A mystical hippie with all the busybody *go, go, go*–ness of a yuppie. She was also a self-proclaimed "white witch"—although I assumed her powers were not particularly strong since she had recently been dumped by her girlfriend and was obsessively scheming and plotting to get her back. The intensity of her co-dependency was so transparent that I couldn't help but wonder, *How can a person who has spent a lifetime in therapy, in twelve-step support groups, not understand or know how to qualify something as basic as co-dependency?*

"Kenny should always put his recovery first. Otherwise he's doomed." I couldn't have agreed with her more and had, for the last two years, completely supported Kenny in his recovery, encouraging him to go to meetings daily, and to seek out a psychiatrist. At the same time, I had never treated Kenny like a powerless child the way his family and friends did, and Nancy was reprimanding me for it.

The lovely thing about being involved with a guy in recovery is that you are always made to feel that his loving you takes his focus off himself—and his recovery. No amount of support, no amount of encouragement for his sobriety can ultimately shake the perception that *you* are taking *him* away from *himself*. It's not much fun competing with your boyfriend for your boyfriend. But for the two years I was living with Kenny, that's exactly what happened.

I knew Kenny was a recovering alcoholic when I met him, I had been in A.A. when I was younger and, because of that, I felt like we understood each other's shadows. When I met him, he talked about God, and Higher Power, and gratitude for life. He knew that his drinking had nearly killed him once and he thanked God that he was sober and had found a supportive lover to boot. I had never felt so much love for another human being than for little Kenny.

As you can possibly surmise from this book thus far—I am not a stranger to people with "issues," myself included. So, when I met Kenny and noticed his flaws, I thought, "He's not perfect. Neither am I? So what!?"

After we moved in together, I began picking up on subtle signs that Kenny had clinical depression. Subtle utterances such as "I think I want to kill myself" would clue me in to his state of mind which, to the untrained ear, might go unnoticed.

Kenny had always suffered with depression, even before I came into the picture. I had grown up with a mother who had a chemical imbalance and whose life was saved by the fabulous new pharmaceuticals on the market.

When I suggested to Nancy that Kenny was obviously chemically depressed and needed to get on meds, she balked.

"There's a lot of angel energy right now on the earth. Yeah, it's the millennium and there are just all these guardian angels amongst us. That angel energy makes people feel really insane."

I regarded her incredulously. She was standing in my kitchen, dressed in her usual pixie/hippie garb, and I realized she was completely serious.

"Um, okay. Well, how does, like, *science* figure into that theory? What about the real problem of brain chemistry, serotonin deficiencies?"

She now looked at me. I could tell what she was thinking: *Angel hater.*

"Craig, this is L.A., we don't believe in science," she laughed, in a way that is not truly laughter.

I returned to my dishes, talking to Nancy with my back to her now.

"Well, it's not that I don't believe in angels. I'm just not a big fan of angels or their energy. If they do exist, I can't really believe in 'guardians' without feeling enslaved by their concern for me—their rules, their nosing into my free will, you know?"

"Wow! You are really—*dark*," Nancy judged, yet in a way so as not to seem truly judgmental. This was not the first time I had been referred to as "dark" by a "spiritual" person. I have been called "dark" many times and I regard the assessment as a form of spiritual racism.

"That's me! The spiritual darkie!" I chirped as I finished drying my last dish.

When you disagree with an "enlightened" person, it's not enough to just say, *Well, live and let live*. Instead they classify you as "dark" or "negative"—someone with dangerous ideas and thoughts to be avoided. My philosophy has always been one of inclusion. If what I say threatens your beliefs, then your beliefs aren't very believable, now are they? But people I have known have built up elaborate walls to keep out voices of dissent and avoid anyone that might have a "conscience"— another word for "dark."

In the mid-1980s I was completely obsessed with New Age spiritualism of the Shirley MacLaine variety. I was an avid *A Course in Miracles* disciple and gobbled up anything I could get my hands on written by Marianne Williamson or Louise Hay. I read up on Buddhism, shamanism, Hinduism, all of the-*isms*.

In other words, in the eighties I was very, well, *eighties*.

Now that the Shirley MacLaine phenomenon is pretty much kaput, I see the loopholes in the tenets of its belief system as well. It occurs to me that it's probably not a good idea to make your guru a self-centered movie actress who is out of touch with reality. Still, at the time, I was fascinated with the occult and looked for limbs to go out on.

My fascination with the occult began in the kitchen of my grandma's double-wide trailer. Nee Naw, my aunt, and my cousins and I stood slack jawed as a jar of Peter Pan peanut butter unscrewed its own lid by itself. We watched, fascinated, as the lid slowly circled until it flopped onto the kitchen table with a metallic *clink*. My grandma, who is one-quarter Cherokee Indian, just stood there, smoking her Carlton, completely calm as the rest of us screamed and backed up against the wall over the Peter Pan peanut butter poltergeist.

"What are you all carryin' on about? It's just a ghost!" Nee Naw puffed. She then ran to the fridge, cig dangling from her mouth.

"What are you doin'?" my aunt Carol asked.

"I'm getting that jar of pickles! The one we can't get the lid off of!"

Nee Naw returned to the kitchen table, setting down the impenetrable jar next to the Peter Pan.

"If we're gonna have a ghost that opens things, we might as well get somethin' outta it!"

Unfortunately for Nee Naw and her arthritic hands, the poltergeist was only interested in peanut butter and never unscrewed another jar again.

Nee Naw was unfazed by any evidence of "the other side." She deeply believed in the mysteries of the universe and had innate psychic abilities. She claimed that her mother, who lived on an Indian reservation, oftentimes visited her after her death. Nee Naw also claimed that when her husband, my mother's father, died in a car accident, she knew the moment it happened even though she was hundreds of miles away. She sat out on the front porch of her house and waited for the police to come and tell her her husband was dead. When they did, she simply said, "I know."

The 1980s New Age movement was most definitely devoid of any pop-psychology influence. If one had a proclivity for being abused, one must have been an abuser in a past life. It had nothing to do with the fact that perhaps one seeks out abuse because one's parents were abusive *in this lifetime*. Once I went into psychoanalysis, I realized that all my mystical beliefs were the result of a complete lack of understanding of human psychology. Psychology had all the answers I had been looking for in in terms of why people do what they do. Mysticism was fun although I realized it was not going to ultimately make me happy.

Since my days ensconced in eighties channeling sessions and healing-crystal conventions, I have suffered at times from a very real and problematic condition—New Age Guilt.

New Age Guilt is based on the tenet that you are the creator of your universe. You create your reality and everything that happens to you, good and bad. Needless to say, having those godlike responsibilities isn't easy for mere mortals to handle. New Age Guilt stems from the assumption that you, somewhere inside your subconscious, brought onto yourself those times when you were robbed, or raped, or betrayed, or got cancer.

Similar to the belief that God punishes us for doubting Him, New Age philosophies say that *you* are God and you are punishing *yourself* for not believing sufficiently in *yourself*. Getting cancer for not believing in yourself seems a little like kicking a dog while it's down, to me. It seems to me that those are the very people who should perhaps not get cancer since just getting out of bed is a chore. Call me crazy.

New Age Guilt has even crept into the thinking of legitimate psychoanalysts. Even my therapist eventually bought into this "blame the victim" philosophy.

I met my first "spiritual guide" in my early twenties.

After being cast in a local play in Dallas, I made friends with a rather odd character named Charlie who was appearing in the production with me. Charlie was a sometime actor, full-time astral projector.

Being that he had no car and lived in a poverty-level apartment complex, Charlie asked if he could catch a ride with me on my daily drives to rehearsal from Dallas. Charlie lived about twenty minutes away from me. His apartment was on the way to Fort Worth, so I happily agreed to pick him up each day.

On these one-hour car rides, Charlie would blab on and on about how he would "astral project" each night. He would claim to leave his body and fly around the sky like Peter Pan.

I would sit in the driver's seat, patiently listening to his incredibly outlandish stories, regretting ever agreeing to drive this kook. Charlie was not your usual astral projector. No crystals hung from his neck, he had no yin/yang tattoos. He lived with a toothless hillbilly woman straight out of *The Grapes of Wrath*, dressed like a cowpoke, wore boots, Wrangler jeans, and spoke with a thick Texan accent. He seemed like a redneck, but the blue streak that came out of his mouth was definitely out of this world.

"I was abducted by aliens when I was a kid. That's when it all began."

"Oh, really?" I humored him. *God, this guy is nuts.*

"Yeah. When you read about the prophecy in the Bible of the Second Coming, what they were describing were space-ships descending from the sky. The thousand years of peace on Earth will be brought by aliens."

"Ahhhh!" I smiled. I had been hearing these New Age delusions for weeks and was growing tired of acting interested.

"Every night I leave my body and float up through the ceiling into my upstairs neighbor's apartment. This black woman lives up there and I'm always seeing her naked and stuff, like getting out of the shower, you know. Of course she has no idea that I'm there."

Okay, he's a pervert on top of everything.

That night, perhaps because he had mentioned seeing his African-American neighbor nude, I had an incredibly vivid sexual dream about a black man. I won't go into what exactly went on between him and me but I did remember that at some point the black man left and Charlie appeared in my dream. While we didn't have sex, I woke up the next day feeling disturbed.

I picked up Charlie at his apartment as usual. He got in the car and smiled at me slyly as we pulled away.

"You have a very lustful mind, don't you?" he grinned.

"Sorry?"

"That dream you had last night—about the black guy."

I nearly drove off the road.

"How did you know that?"

"Well, last night I left my body, and I thought—*I want to see where Craig lives.* You know, when you are out of your body, just the suggestion is all you need and *whoosh!*—you're there. Well, I flew over to your apartment and saw you sleeping at around 4 A.M. While I was there on the Astral Plane, I watched you have your dream."

" 'The Astral Plane'? I thought you said you came to my apartment?"

"The Astral Plane is a carbon copy of our waking reality. You ever gone to bed only to catch your breath, like you're falling, in that second you go to sleep?"

"Yeah."

"Well, that feeling of falling that scares you awake is what it feels like to leave your body. If you work through the fear, you'll be conscious of the separation, like me. Everyone leaves their body when they dream—and those dream experiences happen on the Astral Plane—that's where we go to school and work through our issues."

Suddenly I remembered that I had seen Charlie in my dream that night.

"Wait! You were there. I remember now."

Charlie went on to describe my apartment in detail. He knew I had 80s teal-blue carpeting, he described the contents of my bedroom, even the pictures that were on my bedside table. I lived on the third floor and there was no way Charlie could have seen into my window. We knew no one in common outside the play. He didn't even a know where I lived, and the apartment complex I resided in had a security guard and a gate around the premises anyway.

"Now I feel embarrassed to walk around my apartment naked. You spied on me having sex with some guy on the Astral Plane! That's not nice!"

"It's not like that—when you are outside your body, you have no sexuality. Naked bodies are no different from any other object—like a chair."

"I don't care if I look like a chair naked—don't do that again, for chrissakes!" I yelled.

From that moment on, I began to listen to the far-out Charlie. As far as I was concerned, he had given me proof. Late-night enlightening sessions ensued over coffee at IHOP where Charlie would relate to me all his many travails on the Astral Plane.

"The first time I went to Europa, I was bummed out," he said, pouring ketchup on his Rooty Tooty Fresh and Fruity late-night breakfast.

"Yeah, I've always wanted to go to Paris myself. But only if I'm in love."

"No, not Europe—*Europa*. One night, I left my body as usual and I thought, *I want to go to the nearest planet to Earth that has life on it.* Suddenly, I began flying through space super-fast. I zipped past the moon, the stars became a blur—kinda like 'warp speed' in *Star Trek*. I didn't think I could take it, I was shooting through the solar system so quickly. Finally, I slowed down and saw that I was moving towards a small moon of Jupiter. As I descended, I noticed it was covered with ice and I went through it and underneath the ice was water. These huge kind of crustacean dinosaurs lived there, like big lobsters—not the big-eyed aliens I had expected at all. These creatures weren't intelligent at all."

After our play closed, I lost touch with Charlie. Even though he had the ability to leave his body and go to other planets, Charlie did not have the slightest idea how to live on this planet. He was abused by his smothering and controlling girlfriend, and struggled in poverty, even lived on welfare. Yet he was my very first spiritual guide. That's because he wasn't in it for worldly gain. Not once in his talks of spirituality did he mention utilizing his beliefs to become a movie star. Or to attract money to himself. Or any kind of worldly success. He pursued his spirituality because he was a humble disciple and because he had to. Since then, people I know, myself included at times, pray for riches, pray for fame. Spirituality has become just another way to network—except the net-working is with the angels. *I'll have your people call my people!*

That fateful night when Charlie told me about what he saw on Europa was in February of 1987.

Ten years later, I was in New York City and hadn't thought about Charlie in years. While packing to go to London to shoot a movie, *The Misadventures of Margaret*, I had ABC's *Nightline* on in the background when suddenly I heard the word "Europa."

Rushing to the TV set, I sat down on my bed in disbelief at what I was hearing. NASA's *Galileo* spacecraft had sent back to Earth amazingly detailed images of the surface of Europa. Scientists believe the pictures reveal a relatively young surface of ice, possibly only about a half mile thick in places. Internal heating on Europa due to Jupiter's tidal pull could melt the underside of the icepack, forming an ocean of liquid water underneath the surface. The scientists on *Nightline* surmised that it would not be unreasonable to speculate on the existence of life there. Life on Earth has been discovered at great ocean depths, beyond the penetration of sunlight, thriving on upwelling chemical nutrients from the interior of the planet.

NASA now intends to send a spacecraft to Europa to measure the thickness of the ice and to detect an underlying ocean if it exists; the planned launch date is 2008, with it arriving on Europa in 2010.

Suddenly, everything Charlie had told me over ten years before came screaming back into my mind. So did Arthur C. Clarke's book *2010*, which centers on the moon Europa. While written in 1982, suddenly it seemed as prophetic as the Book of Revelations.

But I do know one thing—NASA can save their money. I know there are gigantic lobsters waiting to be discovered under its icy surface.

I believe that there is something else going on other than what we can see with our eyes. The funny thing is that when I have set aside my life to pursue spirituality, to go to the country, sit still, and contemplate my existence, extraordinary experiences of the supernatural kind cease to exist in my life. It's only when I am living my life to the hilt, falling in love, working, traveling with friends, pursuing my ideas, that spirituality seems to find me as opposed to me finding it. And I like it that way.

During one of my confused sabbaticals to Santa Fe, a place whose spectacular nature scenarios alone could make any atheist think twice, I went to an amazing psychic/astrologer named Georgelle.

At this time in my life, I was very confused about why I was who I was. My acting career had been going very well yet I didn't really understand why I acted. It had all come so easily to me when I was younger and I began to think that acting as a profession was a rather dumb thing to do with one's life. So I went to Santa Fe and sat on a rock for three months.

Georgelle was in her sixties and didn't fit the stereotype of the kiss-ass psychic reader at all—she told it like she saw it, which I loved. She lived modestly in an adobe-type house and had lots of birds everywhere. During the reading the chirping never ceased, like some magical tiki room. Georgelle looked at my chart. She was an amazing presence, formidable and wise and smart.

"Wow, this lifetime is all about career, honey," she said while I drank tea. I only drink tea in situations like this. It is a well-known fact that tea is more "spiritual" than coffee.

"Really? That sucks. What about boyfriends?"

"Uh, nope. Don't see that happening. Sorry, hon. You came to Earth to work this time around."

I was mortified. The whole reason I was in Santa Fe for three months was because I didn't know if I wanted earthly achievements. It seemed shallow. I told Georgelle this.

"Do you know what the word 'career' is derived from?" she asked as she leaned back in her chair. "Taking your 'carriage' down the path. The carriage is you and the path is your life. You can't separate yourself from your career—it is you."

I realized that I had been going on the common assumption that most New Agers succumb to—that certain activities are "spiritual" and others not. How can a gay man afford that kind of morally superior thinking when so much of the world thinks that I am "wrong" just by being alive? If being gay teaches you anything, it's that morality is subjective. You learn that it's all subjective.

I have met people who were incredibly fucked up that I considered deeply enlightened. Similarly I've met people who remind me of fluffy spiritual cats, high above it all, removed from "non-spiritual" emotions like, well, *any* human emotion besides the ones that make you feel numb.

Dropping out of life to sit atop a mountain in a diaper was like dropping out of school and getting my G.E.D. through the mail. Sure you can graduate, but where's the thrill of learning? New Age beliefs may be different, more liberal, but the psychology behind that kind of shutting the world out is exactly like the born-again philosophies I grew up with. It's based in a fear of the "evil" or "negative" world they are es-caping from. Its basic tenet is one of cynicism—a belief that the world is an awful place, or "the devil's playground" as we used to say in church.

The most spiritually evolved people I know don't know they are spiritual. If they were enlightened it happened on the way but was not a destination unto itself.

After my boyfriend's best friend left our apartment, I noticed she had left me a little note, written in sparkly, punky-funky glitter ink. After squinting, trying to figure out what the hell it said, I realized she had written, "Remember Craig, you have your very own angles."

Legitimate Excuses

It used to be that when you ended a meaningful relationship, you had to go to a restaurant or park or some other common place to have a face-to-face talk to say good-bye. In the old days, confrontation was virtually impossible to avoid—there were no phones, no Internet. For those folks afraid of confrontation, there weren't many options but to look into the eyes of the person they were saying good-bye to and have—dare I say it—closure. I've never much liked the term "closure"—some things just can't be closed, certain tragic events. But some things can and need to be closed, especially with eye contact.

The day "I love you" ended, it was replaced with three other words: YOU'VE GOT MAIL!

Cheerily opening an e-mail from my boyfriend, who was out of town, I quickly realized that I had been dumped. Well, not dumped. More like fired. Actually, not even fired—that's too harsh. Instead, I had been laid off.

Andy and I had been living together for the last couple of

years. For over seven hundred days, we had built a life together, spent holidays together, cooked dinners, rented movies, supported each other through hard times, done all the couple things you might see in a movie about couples, if there were such a thing as a movie about gay men in couples. It was the first time in my life I had truly been in love.

"I need to be alone right now," he wrote.

"It's not you. It's me!" He reassured me. Andy's e-mail was expertly written, a model of carefully worded manipulation so as not to give me ammunition of any kind. It obviously had been composed with the help of his newfound therapist, a touchy-feely, drum circle beatin' counselor. His therapist had told Andy that loving me for the last two years was part of a "destructive pattern" and diagnosed him as a "love addict." In her office, I ceased to be a human being and became a "pattern"—and not a pretty one you might see hanging in Martha Stewart's windows: an ugly, destructive pattern—a brown–and–avocado-green plaid, if you will.

I had done my job as boyfriend well, the e-mail continued. He would give me a *glowing* recommendation for my next relationship. You see, the Company of US was downsizing and would no longer require my services; nor would I be allowed to see him anytime soon to have the dreaded "closure." After all these years, I was let go via an e-mail. I was informed, to my surprise, that even though I had been told I was a permanent employee at US, Inc., I was in actuality just a temp. I wasn't even eligible for unemployment benefits.

When you get laid off romantically, there's not a whole lot you can do to argue, especially if the reasons given are peppered with self-help bons mots and faux "empowering" sound bites such as *"I'm not responsible for your feelings,"* or *"I don't love myself, so I can't love you."* Forget that they loved you just fine for years—now they've discovered that how they felt for you during that time was nothing more than emotional indigestion. You were the bad gas that they had finally burped up and didn't like the taste of a second time. Still, I felt comforted knowing that I was not being canned because of any wrong doing of my own. It's not personal, you see. There have been cutbacks here at US, Inc. A romantic recession.

Oh, how I long for the days when people dumped you because they were in love with someone new. You can get angry about that. Nowadays, people get dumped for a torrid affair with one's own self. Andy and I did have one thing in common—we were both involved with the same person: him.

As I was packing my desk in tears, my suddenly ex-boyfriend did allude to reinstating me again at some later time as life partner here at US, Inc. But only when *he* decided that my services would be needed again—once he had "found himself." I thanked him for his generosity and for perhaps keeping me in mind for the future. I did like working here. I felt pride in my job. But I can't pay my rent or bills for a year or more while I hold out for my old position back. And he knows that. He's just letting me down easy.

Andy and I had one of those "soul mate" relationships you read about in women's and teen magazines. According to these sage advice columnists, "soul mate" relationships simply cannot last. There is too much love there and one *must not be entirely in love* in order for a relationship to work long term. It's just like business. *Look out for yourself. Get what you need. Be calm. Be reasonable. Be detached. If you want to move up the ladder, you gotta play the game. Don't lose yourself.*

Confused and begging for some kind of insight into why my lover stopped loving overnight, Andy seemed concerned for me.

"I think you have abandonment issues. You really should look at that," he wrote in a follow-up e-mail.

"I have abandonment issues because I was just abandoned—by you!" I shot back.

Years ago, when someone else I was dating told me early on that they were a "sex addict," I was overjoyed. Good for me! A guy who loves having sex with me! I mean, I am a Scorpio after all.

A month later, when the sex addict casually informed me that he had just gotten fucked in a men's rest stop by a total stranger, he seemed confused by my rather unhappy response.

"I told you—I'm a sex addict! I'm powerless over it. Why are you making this about you, taking this personally? It's my addiction, not yours! God, you really should go to Al-Anon."

Nowadays it seems there is a legitimate excuse for everything: no one's an asshole anymore—people just have "issues." Killers are simply "depressed"; rapists "hate their mothers"; muggers are "addicts" supporting an addiction they are powerless over; sociopaths discard you because they "don't feel worthy of your love." If you have an emotional reaction or feel hurt by all this reckless behavior—you are a codependent and should get thee to Al-Anon.

Today, self-centered "issues" not only go unchecked by society, the asshole-ish act affords the asshole *sympathy*. It's as if the world has become one big "Opposite Day" on *Sesame Street*. If given the slightest provocation, people will gleefully confess what is wrong with them and why. They will effortlessly attach self-diagnostic labels they've heard on TV, like "love addict" or "obsessive compulsive" or "borderline personality," with all the authority of Sigmund Freud himself—even though they have never been in analysis.

Of course, in the past, I have been no different and have

at times listed off my roster of issues as if reciting the day's "specials."

"Hi! My name is Craig and I'll be your self absorbed neurotic today! Today I have fresh anger issues to start off, followed by a delectable sauté of self-loathing with a tasty sexual compulsion on the side. I also have abandonment issues fricasseed with projection. I would offer you a *whine* list but—you just heard it!"

Most of the self-help philosophies I have heard sound good enough to me, I just think they should be falling off the lips of a seventy-five-year-old man or woman who has learned them living a full life. Ultimately I don't buy that a thirty-year-old has earned the right to possess the wisdom of an elder because they've read a self-help book or watched Oprah. It's cheating—the Cliff Notes of the universe. It also makes me wonder, if you have all the answers at thirty where do you go from there? Actually, I know where, because I've seen it happen—you become neurotic, flake out, lose touch with reality because you're ahead of your own game, and start hanging out with the only creatures on earth that can stand you any more: animals.

Over the years, I have dated hairdressers, porn stars, hustlers, writers, graphic artists, nice guys, jerks, drug dealers, cowboys, and Indians. I have dated rich men, poor men, drama queens, stuffy bores, winners, losers, the gifted, and the ungifted.

Now that I am a single gay man traversing the waters of sex in the city again, there are very few things a potential boyfriend might say that would make me drop my fork in a mad dash for a fire exit.

"I've never had a serious relationship," is one.

"I'm not particularly sexual," is another.

"I'm performing in a gay naked musical in the Village"—yet another.

But based on my experience, there is one utterance that absolutely promises a relationship filled with misery, abandonment, and frustration.

That phrase is, *"I like animals more than people."*

Now, I have nothing against animals. I love animals, have always had pets, and I cherish what they bring to my life with all my heart and soul. I have always felt like my pets are my kids. But I do draw the line. I'm ultimately a humanist and while animals are great—you have to admit they *are* a little shallow, albeit in a completely adorable way.

Of course, the sentiment of "up with animals, down with people" is easy to understand. People are jerks. But the two people I've known who preferred the company of animals wound up being the most disappointing humans I'd ever met. I surmised that when they say they love animals, the reason has to be it's because animals love and accept a sociopath, when no self-respecting human being will.

Both of the major relationships of my life ended up as strange miscarriages of love. Both of my exes abandoned the relationship *overnight* after years of living together and, desperate to figure out why, I began looking back for signs I might have missed—something that could have clued me in to the fact that I had been with two different people who had the capacity to shut me off like a light switch after years of being together, without so much as a handshake.

Andy and Ricardo could not have been more different, personality-wise. Yet they did have one thing in common. On my first dates with them, they both told me over dinner that they preferred animals over people.

In our lives we will reject and be rejected, and I have at times been the asshole. I have acted recklessly towards men who loved me, even to Andy and Ricardo. I never expect people to be perfect, myself included, but I do believe in commitment. Ultimately, when a commitment has been made, I will do anything to try and do the work of saving a relationship—go to counseling, schedule sessions with Dr. Phil, exorcisms. The only problem is that I've never been with anyone who also wanted to do the work. Granted, this level of commitment does not apply to "dating"— it's important to delineate the difference between dating someone and actually living with them. Once you live with someone, it's a different ball game entirely.

I had never loved anyone as much as I loved Andy. He was the love of my life. I had been in love before but I had never cherished someone the way I did him. When I was with him, I felt as though I had finally come home. When I was with Andy, my chest literally felt like there was a hole in it. Being in his presence broke my heart in good way.

Our relationship was, before the end, mostly wonderful, and didn't feel at all like an "unhealthy pattern" or "love addiction." We experienced the normal amount of adjustments and obstacles. I learned that love was actually acceptance of the other person, which basically means that no matter how much you annoy each other, you accept that the other person is imperfect and searching, just like you are.

We would see other couples and thank God we weren't them. We had something real and they didn't. Thank God we were us. There would never be the kind of fighting, mistrust, and betrayal that we saw other, less fortunate couples endure. It never occurred to us that other people might be thinking the same thing about us, although I found out later that they were.

One such element of our relationship is that, early on, we fell into the rather disturbing and psychologically transparent habit of talking in baby talk to each other. Not once in a while. For days. Weeks. Years.

"Honey, do you wuv me?"

"Oooh, I wuv you, Andy!"

"Weally? How much do you wuv me?"

"Thhiiiiiisss muuuuuch!"

"Ga ga goo goo bing bong!"

Then quite, unexpectedly, I got pregnant. On November first, I gave birth to a bouncing baby dog—she was a Scorpio, just like me, her mommy. We named her Baby and she was our little angel—the physical manifestation of the adorable-ness of our love.

Wanting to give her the best advantages in this world, we enrolled her in puppy class. Every Tuesday for eight weeks, Baby would learn "sit," "heel," "stay," and other useful tricks a puppy might need to survive in this modern age.

Andy and I took great pride in our dog-ter. She was ob-viously the best of all the puppies. She would always perform her lessons perfectly while the other owners bowed their heads in sorrowful humiliation as Fido peed instead of heeled, when little Spot rolled over instead of sat. Andy and I knew we were lucky parents indeed. Baby was a gifted child.

When we would go grocery shopping it was not uncom-mon for us to notice the many dog models gracing the boxes and cans of the food we purchased for our baby.

"Baby's way cuter than that dog," I would hear myself mutter.

"She could totally be a model," Andy agreed.

As we continued our shopping, visions of Baby on a Milan runway would dance in my head. Sporting the latest Italian trends, she would strut to the end of the runway, serious and brooding, do that little turn on her feet, and whip her tail around as she headed back for her next costume change. I could see it now: fashion spreads in *Vogue*, sharing a bone and a bump with Donatella. Sporting Wayfarers, I could see her backup dancing in Robert Palmer videos. *I am the mother of a dog model. I am the mother of a dog* super*model.*

"She's obviously meant to model, since she was born with eyeliner already applied," Andy commented, while observing her dark eyes.

"I know. Plus the way she sits still while we dress her in outfits, and how she turns her face towards the camera when we take her picture."

"She definitely knows her *good side*," Andy nodded.

I saw Baby's career laid out before me. There would be the inevitable fluff piece in *People* magazine where Baby, in her Hollywood home, barks on and on about the hardships of staying thin, her new line of fur-care products, and her romance with aging screen icon Beethoven.

My fantasy came to a crashing halt one day. After scouring Los Angeles pet stores looking for dog clothing, preferably something with sequins, I stopped the car. *What was I doing?* Suddenly I realized that Baby was Jon-Benet and *we* were John and Patsy Ramsey. And we all know how well that worked out.

I told Andy we needed to let Baby have a choice in the matter.

"But you've seen how she loves having her picture taken. She *works* the camera," he reminded me. "She wants to be a dog model! *She does!*" he cried as he threw himself on our bed, his face buried in his arms sobbing.

"I know, honey, I know."

We decided not to put Baby through the pressures of dog modeling at such an early age and instead opted to allow her a normal puppyhood. If she wanted to pursue modeling at a later date, it would be her decision and I would support her in any endeavor she committed herself to.

Except an acting career. That, I would definitely discourage her from pursuing.

Soon after that, Andy had started to favor Baby's company over mine. Eventually, my capacity to love my boyfriend would be compared to the drooling adoration a dog could give him. Any time I stated a romantic need of mine, he would just look at Baby wistfully and think, *Why can't Craig love me the way you do?*

Having a dog is rather like having a slow child. I have always looked at the parents of dumb children and marveled at their seemingly endless capacity to love. I always wondered if I had the same untapped capacity to love in me as well. Then I got a dog and realized I did. Like most parents of dumb children, I dug deep and, although there were times when I wanted to drop-kick her across Tenth Avenue, I loved her. I was comforted by the number of other parents at the many dog parks I frequented. There we all were, the mommies and daddies of our furry babies, who were all the cuter for their low IQ's.

But alas, Baby was just another statistic in the long run. She became a child of divorce. She eventually no longer represented Andy and my adorable love, but became a living breathing testament to his inability to love me the way he loved a dog.

A few weeks after Andy had left me, I told my mother what had happened.

"Good God, not again! I just don't understand it! Why can't you find somebody to stay with you!?"

This might sound somewhat harsh, but it's completely true. I've been dumped before—a lot.

"Well, you sound like you are dealing with this well—at least you have your book to write."

I didn't tell my mother that I was actually not writing, but still in bed, lovesick, going on my third week of Camille-like consumption, addicted to AMC and Turner Classic Movies in a desperate search for "simpler times." I'm certain I have now seen every Hollywood film made before 1963. It's amazing how the only criterion for "classic" status is that a movie be over forty years old.

"Yeah, well. It gets harder to stay romantically optimistic when you're thirty-five and still wrestling with a complete inability to settle down with someone," I moaned as I stuffed an entire Entenmann's marshmallow cake into my mouth.

"You have the worst taste in men!"

"I know. I don't have *affairs*—I have a-*circuses*."

"I thought you and Andy were going to get married!" she sighed. "He proposed to you, gave you a ring! I just don't understand you gays!"

And I don't blame my mother one bit for that comment. I don't understand gays much more than she does, and I go down on them.

Andy had indeed proposed marriage to me after our first year of living together.

He would say things like, "I know you're the one," and, "I want to grow old with you." I later found out that what he really meant was, "I know you're the one—*today*," or, "I want to grow old with you—*this afternoon*."

Still, at the time I believed him, and didn't say yes right away. I wanted to make sure that if we got married, I was really ready for that. As soon as I started talking about doing it, talked about what songs we'd play at our wedding, honeymooning in Paris, he flipped out and used his "get out of relationship free" card, deciding he had "issues."

I know that I should be lobbying my congressman to get a gay marriage bill passed in my state, but secretly I pray that no such opportunity will ever exist for me.

This is because if gays could get married, I would be the Liz Taylor of gay matrimony. With each successive boyfriend, I have been convinced he is "the one" and if I could legally run off to Las Vegas, I'm sure I would have been married at least six times by the age of thirty-five. The divorces that would have followed, the child support for the various cats and dogs and birds that I have lost custody of, would have moved me into a refrigerator box in Central Park. Basically, gay marriage, to me, means gay divorce and gay divorce lawyers.

The e-mails from Andy continued, since his therapist had told him not to talk to me either on the phone or in person and to rely on that nifty and swifty tool of virtual communication. There he wouldn't be burdened with an actual discourse or dialogue, and could make his statements clear without my involvement or feedback. He was, however, willing to call me in New York City on the hideous day that was September 11, 2001.

The e-mail breakup had only been a month before. The day that my beloved city was attacked by terrorists, most of us New Yorkers thought, *This is it*. We had no idea whether the next ball was going to drop. Rumors of potential anthrax, exploding gas mains, and neutron bombs wagged on tongues. I sat in my apartment with my cat, Junior, watching television—and missing my boyfriend more than ever. I had called him several times only to discover that he was on a camping trip. When he finally did call me back, it was late in the night. Finally, we were able to speak on the phone. No e-mails. Person to person. My potential obliteration had superceded his therapist's suggestions of not speaking to me. I was about to get closure on the one day I didn't want it.

"I just wanted you to know that regardless of us breaking up a month ago, I really did love you, Andy. You were the love of my life. Today I was afraid that I was going to die. I knew people who did die today and I was just sitting here, realizing that life is so short and fragile, and it's at times like this that you realize how stupid petty disagreements and resentments are. So I called my parents in Texas and told them that I loved them. Just in case another plane blew up or some strange plague broke out here. I felt compelled to call you and tell you the same thing—that I love you, in spite of us not being able to be together. I wanted you to just know that I love you and always will in my heart," I cried into the phone.

Andy sighed.

"Craig," his intonation was as if wearily reprimanding an old woman, "I don't love you anymore and I'm uncomfortable with where you are taking this conversation."

As I sat in my Hell's Kitchen tenement, bleary-eyed from crying and lack of sleep, drunk on adrenaline, I realized how pathetic this moment was.

No more. Here I was pining away for someone who supposedly loved me for two years, yet who decided to tell me for the first time that they no longer loved me in the midst of disaster on the darkest night of my life. Andy had ended our relationship via e-mail, but he chose September 11, 2001, to make himself perfectly clear.

So many people had died that day not far from my house, so many people had lost their significant others in heroic acts of bravery, and here I was dealing with the worst possibly timed rejection of my life. The people that perished trying to save others could have used "legitimate excuses" to not go into a burning building. They could have said, "I don't love myself enough to love anyone else today," or, "I'm not responsible for other people's feelings." In one day I saw the worst in humankind and the best, both in my city and also in the people closest to me. I saw great generosity of spirit in my friends and mind-blowing callousness in my lover. But it wasn't his fault. He just had issues. In fact, he had a subscription. I didn't take my grandma's advice and throw the shit back that day. I was too tired of mudslinging and games. I wasn't mad. From that day on, I became intolerantly bored with people's personal dramas. Including my own.

Another thing happened to me that day. I suddenly preferred the company of animals over people. Animals didn't have intimacy issues or fear of commitment. They didn't even know how to type to send you an e-mail. They didn't do things like blow up thousands of people because they have tiny dicks or because of some stupid religious conviction. They love you anyway. They love you because they are, like myself, very dumb children.

Robert Reed

I'm no role model. I use the "F" word, don't work out, eat red meat, and have been known to wear white after Labor Day. I've had one-night stands, done drugs, and cheated on my boyfriends. I tried being a positive gay role model for about forty-five minutes in 1995 because, well, I forgot that I was a human being. However, I'm a *real* model. I make you feel mighty real.

Several years ago, I did a film called *Frisk*. Now, the film had its faults—some sucky performances, bad pacing, and low budget-itis. Despite its shortcomings though, *Frisk* aimed to be about something—self-loathing. How do you execute a film addressing the very real issue of gay self-loathing without having self-loathing gays in it? Well, according to politically correct gays who would rather turn a blind eye to faulty gay people, you don't make the film at all.

Everyone should experience, once in their life, the pleasure of having fifteen hundred people boo you off a screen during a nude scene. *Frisk* had premiered at San Francisco's Gay and

Lesbian Film Festival in the fabulous Castro Theater. Just moments after applauding a tribute for *Frisk*'s producer, Marcus Hu, my movie began. Since the lead character was gay and talked about how being a sexual outlaw eventually led to his being a *real* outlaw—and consequently a killer—the audience lost it. They wanted to see lovable gays with no problems up there, preferably with a few shirtless hunks thrown in. I sat in the balcony as fifteen hundred people booed the movie and threw popcorn and pride rings at the screen. Never mind the fact that I believe my work in *Frisk* is my best. "Positive Role Models," you see, have been more important to some audiences than good acting.

Why gay people would want something that has been proven to be a myth to everyone else still baffles me. We all know that *Leave It to Beaver* was familial propaganda—that *The Brady Bunch* was a lie. We all grew up in dysfunctional families and felt extra gypped when we compared our realities with those perfect family fantasies we saw on TV. Those role models turned out to be an untruth and in the process, disenfranchised a generation and caused rebellion in the sixties by young people who felt those American Myths had made them feel even worse about themselves than they would have if the Cleavers had never existed. The Cleavers weren't real. Or at least to the majority of people in this country.

I discovered *The Brady Bunch* was a lie when I was seven—at the height of the show's popularity. My Grandma Gay, Nee Naw, worked as Communications Manager at Huntington Hospital in Pasadena, California, which basically meant that she managed the switchboard. While I was visiting her at Christmas, Nee Naw came home from work one day and lighting up her usual Carlton and putting a pot of coffee on, I remember overhearing her tell my mother and my aunt

Carol that Robert Reed, Mr. Brady of *The Brady Bunch*, had been admitted to the hospital that day with a Coke bottle lodged in his butt.

Now, back then, Coke bottles were much smaller than they are today, just to cut Mr. Reed some slack. My mom and aunt couldn't repress their snickering. At age seven, I wasn't sure how he'd got a Coke bottle up there, but I could tell from their reactions that it was reason for him to be embarrassed.

A few years later I had my first sexual relationship. Not with a man, not with a woman, but with a deodorant.

"Mom! My Tickle smells funny!" my sister cried.

Sitting on my bed, I froze.

"What?" my mother yelled back.

"I think my Tickle fell in the cat box!"

I sat and waited for the sounds of my mother's footsteps approaching the bathroom in which my sister was standing. Across the hall, my mother would enter the bathroom, examine my sister's Tickle deodorant and it would all be over.

For weeks I had been using my sister's Tickle deodorant bottle for purposes other than sweaty armpits. Tickle was strong enough for a man but made for a woman and I should know because it had turned me into one.

Along with Andy Gibb's hairy-chested album cover, Tickle and I really had something going there for a while. Tickle was always there, utterly reliable and never said it had a headache. Tickle and Andy were in on my little Secret—a name brand of deodorant that I had to sadly break up with, since it was the epitome of a square peg.

That is until now. Now we were discovered. I remembered when my mom had heard about Robert Reed and how she had laughed at him along with my aunt. I could see her laughing at me as well.

I'm like Mr. Brady, I thought. I'm bad. *But how can that be? Mike Brady is good.* Suddenly, I made the connection. Mr. Brady stuck a Coke bottle up his butt because he liked it! Just like me!

As it all came together, I realized that the Coke bottle Robert Reed had stuck up his butt was a shameful and nasty secret. The same way I felt shameful and nasty—yet something in me told me it wasn't wrong. That it was just how I was. How Robert Reed and I were.

The moment I realized that Robert Reed was gay was the moment I realized that I was, too. It was also the moment I realized that what I saw on TV didn't have anything to do with real life. I realized that it was a big act, that there is no such thing as a Mike Brady. He was a silly fantasy, someone without an asshole altogether! There was, however, such a thing as Robert Reed, a man who had secrets and who liked sticking things up in his butt.

Eventually I overcame my shame. I came out and found other reasons to have empathy for Robert Reed and what his life must have been like, having to hide the very real desires of a fully grown, gay man's complicated life and at the same time be contractually obligated be a "positive role model" to millions of children and fathers out there.

Although I wanted to be an actor, I promised myself I would never put myself in the position of having to be something I'm not. Or to participate in a lie. Even as an openly gay actor, I have to fight that. Because now, God help us, we have positive *gay* role models to mess us up all over again.

The very phrase "role model" implies that there is a role to play. Playing a role implies that it's a performance, acting. And that implies that it's fiction, not real. The reason I don't believe in positive role models is because I don't know who it is, exactly, that determines what falls under "positive" or "negative." There are obvious negative traits a person might possess, like perhaps the need to kill people and eat them, or the practice of throwing puppies off roofs, but otherwise, I don't want some group, Christians or gay activists, telling me what to say or think or be. At the same time, aside from puppy killers, I don't want to imply that I don't strive for high-minded ideals. I'm completely against collectivism. I am, in my heart, an individualist. I believe in the rights of the individual over the rights of any community or cause. I'm aware of the political power wielded by collectivism. But aside from it as a political necessity, I think any community that is not made up of freethinking individuals is destined to be oppressed by its own members.

I suppose it's radical of me to suggest that it might be possible for a community—gay, black, Asian, or Himalayan mulatto midgets—to encourage personal individuality and still find enough of a reason to have a beer bust or a tea dance. The gay community is so diverse; yet you wouldn't know that if you turned only to movies and TV for enlightenment.

While African-American moviegoers have begged for three-dimensional portrayals of themselves, eschewing stereotypes like "Stepin Fetchit" and "Mammy" roles, the gay community has actually gone in reverse. We were offered thought-provoking queer cinema in the mid-1990s that represented complex gay characters, in movies like *Poison*, *Grief*, *David Searching*, *Prick Up Your Ears*, *Edward II*, et cetera, but due to organizations like GLAAD and Queer Nation, those complex gay characters were written off as "negative role models." Thanks to their efforts, we have now become as bland as *The Brady Bunch*—and one-dimensional.

The Gay and Lesbian Alliance Against Defamation sounds

like a good idea. I mean I'm all for an organization that makes overpaid breeders like Mel Gibson stop and think before rattling off some locker-room joke about how many gays can fit on a bar stool. But, like most things, something good can easily become just another form of oppression—especially to artists and freethinkers.

I am one of a handful of actors in American cinema who are openly gay (with the ranks growing daily, thank God) yet I have never, not once, been invited to a GLAAD function, even though I have worked almost exclusively in gay cinema. The reason is because I have not made many films in my ten-year career that fit the "positive role model" requirement to garnish a GLAAD stamp of approval (*Swoon*, gay killers; *Frisk*, gay druggies and killers; *I Shot Andy Warhol*, lesbians with guns; *Kiss Me, Guido*, promiscuous gay man).

It doesn't matter to them that I am an outspoken actor who has made tremendous professional sacrifices to be "out." Or that I have a mind of my own and that I have committed my life to demanding that gays and lesbians be treated the same as everyone else. That doesn't make me a positive role model. Being that they are not an organization run by artists, but activists, they suffer from an innate inability to separate an artist from his work. They are a non-creative organization relegating creativity and are conservative to boot.

A couple of years ago, I was asked to be on an MSNBC panel about being gay in Hollywood. I had recently been dubbed the "King of Queer Cinema" and was on my fifth gay movie at the time. *The Birdcage* had just become a huge hit at the box-office and I was brought on the show to discuss how I thought this would affect the perception of gay people at large. I would appear with Bruce Steele, an editor at *Out* magazine who later moved to *The Advocate*, and Liz Manne, who worked for a distribution company and later went on to head the Sundance Channel.

While waiting in the greenroom with the fabulous and evolved Bruce and Liz, we were introduced to a woman who would also appear on the show. A woman from GLAAD.

After formal introductions, we all nervously voiced our opinions before going in front of the cameras. The show was live, which made us all scared.

The woman from GLAAD, however, was a total pro. She seemed a nice enough person, albeit a little robotic.

"I'm going to endorse *The Birdcage*," she said in a clipped, enunciated tone.

"Really?" I said, genuinely surprised. I thought there might be someone on the show endorsing this movie, but had assumed it would be an employee of Paramount, who made the film, and had been ordered to go and defend the film against any dissidence.

The MSNBC producers told us that we might also discuss *Philadelphia*—a film that actually moved me because I thought it showed very clearly how a straight man deals with the conflict between his homophobia and his heart. I thought it was psychologically sound. I appreciated the fact that Tom Hanks's character was portrayed as a flawed man who got HIV sucking off a stranger in a porn theater while cheating on his lover—a reality of gay couples I knew in real life. But *The Birdcage* was not real life—just cartoonish. Granted, it was a comedy, but it gave people a chance to laugh at asexual gay men—a phenomenon not new to American cinema, as so beautifully illustrated in Vito Russo's *The Celluloid Closet*.

Of course, Hollywood has also had a penchant for gay villains, psychos, and other gay degenerates. I'm not for that either. In my mind, a gay character is redeeming only if he or she is three-dimensional. When I see a gay character that is a one-dimensional killer or a one-dimensional butt of a joke, that's what is offensive to me. Like everything else in life, the intention behind the character is what should be judged. If the intention of the movie or TV show is to help us understand what makes a three-dimensional gay character tick, then it's illuminating, it's art, and should be left alone by watchdog groups no matter how badly that character may be behaving in their eyes.

I still find that America has no problems with gay people as long as they make them laugh or do their hair and decorate their homes. Just like blacks, we are allowed to eat at the table as long as we're entertaining or useful.

"Didn't you find Robin Williams and Nathan Lane unbelievable as lovers? I mean did you really believe that they had a sexual relationship?" I asked the lady who was GLAAD *The Birdcage* existed.

"The film made money and we think that's great for gay people," she said with all sincerity.

Then there is the issue I like to call "Pink Face." It's a different version of Black Face, where a white actor pretends to be black to comic effect. I, as an openly gay actor, often lose gay roles to straight actors, because I am not "gay" enough. I've also been told, amazingly, that the producers of a TV show I was up for needed to cast a straight actor in the leading gay role, so that people at home would know it was "all just pretend."

Hollywood executives seem to think, ever since *Ellen*, that if they cast someone who is openly gay in a gay role, that actor will use the show as a platform for their "gay agenda." Never mind that every single other show has pushed its straight agenda—from *Melrose Place* to *Home Improvement* to *Happy Days*—for years. As a result, a lot of straights play gays to show off their amazing acting range. People seem to think that every gay show that pops up now is some form of gay charity work, and it's not. Hollywood is about money.

If *Will & Grace* weren't a huge hit, this wouldn't be happening. I happen to like *Will & Grace* and think it's incredibly clever. Yet when I hear that one of the actors on the show is gay and yet not out of the closet, I have to ask myself, "If you can't be out on *Will & Grace*, then what actor can?" Gay characters have always been in entertainment. Audiences have always laughed at them. That's nothing new historically. But if a gay actor can play an empowered, out gay man on a TV show and not be one in his real life for fear of the repercussions, then what has truly changed in the world? It's not the actor's fault that climate exists. It's everyone's.

What gay people are, however, is complex. The very fact that we are not allowed to be complex or multidimensional in movies and TV is another unrealistic standard to live up too and another form of self-oppression. We're more interested in acquiring mainstream America's acceptance than being honest or true about where our strengths *and* our weaknesses lie, and we have lost our souls in the process.

GLAAD's real issue is not with a gay/straight thing but with a moral thing. It's tied into Judeo-Christian ideas of good and bad behavior. Who says drag queens or dykes on bikes make us look bad? Who says sleeping around is bad if you don't hurt anyone? Don't people, gay and straight, act out from time to time? It's human and real and therefore beautiful. If we can learn something about Leopold and Loeb and how their sexuality played a part in their co-dependency, then shouldn't we? Shouldn't a gay person who's struggled with addictions and self-loathing—like my character in *Frisk*—have a voice? How can we as a gay community feel ashamed about being faulted and human? The very nature of that censorship lies in self-loathing, which is the irony. Not just gay self-loathing, but loathing of their own flawed humanity.

Since the demise of the "New Queer Cinema" the power structure of GLAAD has changed hands, and their current incarnation is more temperate. However, the potential backlash to standards of gay wholesomeness is yet to be seen. When you set a standard of perfection for gay teens to live up to—if young gay people only see perfect gay people with perfect gay bodies and affluent gay lifestyles on TV and in movies—they will feel inadequate in their real-life imperfections in their humanity, and feel worse about themselves as a whole than ever. If there is such a thing as the gay "Cleavers" someday, the comparisons and let downs from that unrealistic standard will cause the same backlash as the original "Cleavers." The same way role models have let us down before. Role models are not the truth but an ideal and, just like *The Brady Bunch*, a well-intentioned lie but a lie nonetheless.

Similarly, I'm not advocating a division between gay people. We are not each other's enemy, or at least we shouldn't be. It's a very precarious line to walk: to maintain your values, speak your individual truth, and hope that gay people who disagree with you also hear what you are saying and not take it personally. It's also a difficult thing to discuss very real issues about representation and not come across like a sour grapes actor. But I believe that gay people can disagree on certain issues, that we can exist as a collective of individuals, and still know that we all ultimately want the same thing—to be happy, to be left alone to love who we want, and to be free, even if our ideas about how to get there may be different or even sometimes opposed.

Years later, when I read that Robert Reed had died of AIDS, I noticed that he had died in Pasadena. At my Nee Naw's old place of employment—Huntington Hospital. Have a Coke and a smile for him.